Making Your Phone Ring
with Internet Marketing
for Cemeteries

Making Your Phone Ring
with Internet Marketing
for Cemeteries

Welton Hong

Founder of Ring Ring Marketing®
www.RingRingMarketing.com

This book and the information contained herein are for informative purpose only. The information in this book is distributed on an "As Is" basis, without warranty. The author makes no legal claims, express or implied, and the material is not meant to substitute legal or financial counsel.

The author, publisher, and/or copyright holder assume no responsibility for the loss or damage caused, or allegedly caused, directly or indirectly by the use of information contained in this book. The author and publisher specifically disclaim any liability incurred from the use or application of the contents of this book.

All rights reserved. No part of this book may be reproduced or transmitted in any form by any means, electronic, mechanical, photocopying, recording, or otherwise, without the prior written permission of the author or publisher.

Throughout this book trademarked names are referenced. Rather than putting a trademark symbol in every occurrence of a trademarked name, we state that we are using the names in an editorial fashion only and to the benefit of the trademark owner with no intention of infringement of the trademark.

Copyright © 2021 Welton Hong
All Rights Reserved

Printed in the United States of America

ISBN: 978-1-7378591-0-9

Thanks to my parents Shunhua and Sumei for their guidance, my wife Ihsuan for just about everything, and to my siblings William and Jennifer who make it all worthwhile.

I'd also like to thank David Shipper, President & CEO of Indiana Memorial Group, for providing insight and assistance.

TABLE OF CONTENTS

INTRODUCTION	**1**
SECTION 1: LEAD GENERATION	
Chapter 1: Search Engine Marketing (SEM)	**19**
Pay Per Click Advertising (PPC)	**21**
Local Search Optimization	**40**
Search Engine Optimization (SEO)	**54**
Chapter 2: Mobile Marketing	**72**
Chapter 3: Social Media Marketing (SMM)	**84**
SECTION 2: CONVERSIONS	
Chapter 4: Maximizing Website Conversions	**115**
SECTION 3: REVIEWS AND REPUTATION	
Chapter 5: Customer Review Sites and Reputation Management	**151**
Chapter 6: Email Marketing	**171**
SECTION 4: MONITORING AND MEASURING	
Chapter 7: What Gets Measured Gets Done	**185**
SECTION 5: WORKING WITH A MARKETING PROFESSIONAL	
Chapter 8: Finding a Qualified, Principled Internet Marketing Professional	**199**
CONCLUSIONS	**213**

INTRODUCTION

For most of the past decade, my complete focus has been helping deathcare professionals succeed by harnessing the power of internet marketing.

To that end, my team at Ring Ring Marketing (which comprises more than 100 full-time marketing professionals as of this writing) and I keep looking for ways to innovate in this field.

We're always striving to find new ways to help businesses grow, generate sales more efficiently, and overcome challenges.

It's true that most of our deathcare clients to date run funeral homes. And without question, there are differences in how funeral homes and cemeteries generate sales and market themselves.

With that said, the more I've talked with cemetery owners over the past couple of years, the more I've realized how many aspects of digital marketing fit this field so well.

As of 2021, we've reached the point where if you're not marketing your business on the internet, you're essentially not marketing yourself at all. And yes, that's still true for highly traditional businesses such as cemeteries.

I'm not saying you shouldn't do any "offline" marketing; in fact, I strongly encourage it! Any marketing approach that delivers positive ROI is a good one.

However, I definitely look at offline marketing now as more of an "added complement" to online marketing. It's more than a garnish, but it's not much more than a side dish to the entrée that is internet marketing.

For for-profit cemeteries, digital marketing provides an opportunity to broaden your audience. It helps you generate trust and high perceived value in your facilities and services.

Another great thing about investing in online marketing for a cemetery is that most public cemeteries remain well behind the 8-ball in marketing their services on the internet.

In other words, odds are that your local competitors probably aren't doing too much online. They might have a half-decent website that looks okay but hasn't been updated technologically in 10 years. I see that a lot.

They might have a pinky toe in social media—most likely a Facebook page that's rarely updated—but that's it. I also see *that* a lot.

As a quick example, as I'm writing this in fall of 2021, I'm looking at the FB page for a local cemetery (the competitor of an RRM client).

The most recent post on its feed is from March 2019, a full *two years ago*. It's a request for donations. When I flipped through the previous two dozen posts, they were all the same thing: requests for donations.

That's it. There's no content to engage and inform potential clientele. And when any business's most recent FB post is over two years old, anyone viewing its page is most likely to conclude this entity is no longer in business! (It's not, but that's the impression it's providing.)

Of course, the worst thing you can do when you're on social media is just stop posting. It's far worse than never having had an account in the first place! This particular cemetery would be better off closing its Facebook account than just letting it lie there comatose for two-plus years.

Granted, many cemeteries do a much better job of marketing themselves on social media. But many more do just as bad a job, or worse.

And hey, I get it. Certain business types seem less aligned with social media than others, and most cemetery owners likely don't see the point in engaging in a robust social media campaign.

In truth, social media can be extremely powerful for cemetery marketing, because it's the best option for overall branding and for educating potential clientele. There's *massive opportunity* for whichever cemetery in a given area takes the reins on social media.

That cemetery should be **yours**. You should be taking the lead and branding yourself as the public cemetery in your area. You should have the best website, one that truly shows off your cemetery grounds, your mausolea and columbaria, your cremation garden, and so on.

Your cemetery should be showing off how it's different from the other available options, hammering its **unique selling proposition (USP)** at every turn.

Your cemetery should be the one collecting lots of five-star reviews on platforms such as Google, Facebook, and Yelp.

Great reviews are the big difference makers for today's consumers, particularly in this post-COVID era when so many middle-aged and older people have become far more accustomed to researching service options online.

The fact that so many independent cemeteries have invested little in digital marketing isn't a reason to avoid it — it's all the more reason to make your mark now! It's like an untapped market just waiting for you to take advantage. By acting first, you can completely dominate your market, even becoming a relatively household name (at least for an interested segment of the audience) in your geographic area.

To succeed, you need to intelligently *reinvest your capital* in marketing methods that consistently produce greater revenue. Many techniques I detail in this book achieve exactly that result.

And again, while digital marketing is my chief area of expertise, I remain a fan of any offline marketing effort that generates revenue for your cemetery.

That could be the print Yellow Pages. It could be a local directory. It could be a direct mail campaign.

Depending on the particulars of your area, it could even be billboards, bus bench advertising—you name it. *If it's working for you, do it.*

You don't have to drop all the "old-school" methods just because digital has taken over so much of how we do business today.

But...

(You knew there was going to be a *but*, right?)

But…the reality is that the vast majority of print directories go straight into recycling bins in 2021. Many such directories aren't even printed anymore, because there's so little value in even producing them.

Today, essentially everyone has a smartphone, including preteens, great-grandparents, and everyone in between. Many Americans have a smartphone *and* at least one tablet. Many also have other devices to conveniently access the internet 24/7.

The past few holiday seasons brought American households a ton of *smart speakers*: incredibly user-friendly devices that sit on counters and tablets. You can get information just by calling out to Google or Alexa or Siri (or Amazon for retail needs).

Which means if someone needs immediate information on burial or cremation, all they need to do is call out to the speaker for a local recommendation.

It's that easy now. You don't even have to get out of your chair and fish out the Yellow Pages. You can even place a call to a cemetery without even grabbing your phone.

The cemeteries getting those calls? They're the ones that *optimized* their businesses for that purpose. Which is a basic element of digital marketing.

You might be thinking that most of the families who contact you probably still aren't getting information through a smart speaker. That's true. It might be another several years until that technology reaches widespread adoption.

But you *do* know many that will go straight to the internet for information. That's been the trend for years now, and again — yes, you'll hear this a lot — it's especially true in 2021.

They might go to a desktop computer to do a search. They might also reach for a convenient tablet. And it's entirely possible that they'll simply pick up their phone. Why not? They can simply use their voice to do a search on their phone (much like a smart speaker). Or they might just type in their search.

Either way, simply asking for "local cemetery" or "cemetery near me" or even just "cemetery"—search engines such as Google know where you are, after all, and will just search locally anyway—will immediately pull up local listings.

If you've done your due diligence with search engine optimization (SEO), you'll be at the top of those listings. (Or at least *near* the top, if you're in an especially competitive area.) If you haven't, you won't get those calls.

Of course, the other obvious benefit to a smartphone is that it's entirely portable. You always have the internet right at your fingertips, no matter where you are or what time it is.

So if you're away from home — even thousands of miles away — and you suddenly find yourself immediately needing burial or cremation services, it's no problem at all. You just reach for your phone.

You can access a cemetery in a matter of seconds.

Thanks to click-to-call technology, you can be *on the phone with a cemetery professional with a single tap*.

That's how easy it is. And a family in need can be contacting your cemetery that way—*if* you've optimized for mobile.

If you haven't, some other cemetery is getting that call.

In his 2017 book *The Truth About Your Future*, renowned financial advisor Ric Edelman wrote about how rapidly technology has been changing everything about American life:

> *[T]o understand what your future will be like, you need to understand why it's going to be so radically different from what you have been assuming. The reason is technology. And not just ordinary technology but exponential technologies—innovations that are advancing at rates of exponential growth.*

Edelman goes on at length about exponentiality at Moore's Law, but I'll try to simplify it for you:

If you think things have changed a lot the last few years, just wait. Due to exponential technologies, they're going to move *much* more rapidly over the next few years.

That's why I'm concerned for cemeteries that are slow to adapt to these changes in 2021 — and some aren't adapting at all.

Sitting tight and doing things "the way they've always been done" simply isn't going to work anymore. That ship has already sailed.

If cemetery professionals put their head in the sand and pretend the world isn't rapidly changing, they aren't going to grow. Heck, they're not even going to maintain the level of business they have *now*. They're just going to keep losing interments and revenue as the world changes around them.

If what I'm saying sounds scary…good! That means I'm doing my job. I need you to understand what you're dealing with. I need you to realize how imperative it is that you don't wait another second to evolve.

I run a pay-for-results business. Here's what that means: **If you don't make money, I don't make money**. At Ring Ring Marketing, I've always operated with the mindset that *your success is our success*.

I wouldn't have it any other way. That's how I was raised. I'm not going to accept your money if I can't take that investment and turn it into significant revenue generation for your business.

That's why RRM has a 100 percent money-back guarantee for a full 60 days. My business *depends* on the cemeteries and funeral homes I partner with making money.

So I can't afford to beat around the bush. I have to be honest about the challenges you're facing. I can't pretend you have all the time in the world to get around to accepting the digital revolution and prioritizing online marketing for your cemetery.

That's why I have to cut to the chase:

Things are changing incredibly rapidly right now, and if you *don't act very soon, you'll be left behind.*

The change was on the horizon when personal computers became standard in people's homes. But the big turn, the first one, occurred when a 24/7 internet connection became more common than not.

That's when people realized they could just as easily jump on their computers and look up listings for local businesses without breaking out the phone book. And as more and more businesses invested in websites and listings on Google and similar sites, specific information about those businesses became available.

Businesses could provide much more information (at no extra cost) on their sites and listings than they ever could in a Yellow Pages listing or ad. Customer reviews, hours of business, recent testimonials — all of that and more was available to potential customers whenever they liked.

That was the status quo for a while, but another big sea change occurred over just the past decade with two great technological innovations: smartphones and tablets.

It's one thing to be able to access information from around the world in the comfort of your home. It's something else entirely to have that information available in the palm of your hand, 24 hours a day, no matter where you are: at the coffee shop, in the park, in your car.

As of 2021, smartphones are now far more powerful than a top-of-the-line personal computer used to be. The same is true of tablets. And with increases in speed and download power, it's now incredibly easy for someone with only the most basic understanding of technology to access all this information in seconds.

Many businesses have taken advantage of this by optimizing their websites and listings for mobile technology. While your type of business has some obvious differences from retail or traditional service industries, the differences are not as great as you might think.

Even in deathcare, the way to connect with those who would purchase your services is increasingly becoming an online process.

That's just the reality in 2021, when many people have moved on from print advertising and exclusively determine their service providers by going online.

And while that might sound like a purely generational thing ("only Generation Z or maybe millennials do that"), it's not true.

Generation X has shown virtually *no* allegiance to print advertising in this digital age. And in 2021, even many baby boomers are more likely to get information from their desktop computers or (even more likely) tablets and smartphones than from the Yellow Pages, or a newspaper (many of which are also on the brink of extinction), or any other print product.

That's how much things have changed.

A few years ago, many of the websites you pulled up on your smartphone would be hard to read or even unintelligible, because those sites had been created to be viewed on a large computer monitor.

That's no longer the case. The most successful sites now appear in mobile versions that look perfectly fine on everything from a tablet to even a small smartphone.

(Yours must be too, which I'll cover later when we talk about having a **mobile-friendly website**.)

The key to this transition: No longer are only the young or the especially tech-savvy looking for product or service information on their phones or tablets.

Now, *everyone*, from a preteen to a great-grandmother, can do this quickly and easily. That's how far the technology has improved in a short time.

That's why the print Yellow Pages are virtually extinct now, and types of print advertising from newspaper ads to magazines are continuing to plummet in reach and effectiveness.

In 2021, the term "marketing" means, for the most part, "internet marketing."

Yes, some offline methods still work, but if you're not marketing your business on the internet in today's world (even in the deathcare industry, comparatively traditional as it is), you're virtually invisible to a huge swath of potential customers.

The difference between 2010 and 2015 was huge. The difference between 2015 and 2021 is *enormous*.

As the owner of a cemetery, you have a number of potential marketing outlets available to you, but in today's digital age, one thing is irrefutable:

If you're not promoting yourself online, you're losing critical exposure with every month that passes.

Most people investigating deathcare services skew older than the average consumer. The industry itself is more traditional than most.

Yes, those are both true. Unfortunately, they're also too often used as excuses for why cemeteries fail to market themselves as aggressively online as they should.

The transition from print to digital has affected members of every generation, even those who grew up without 24/7 internet or even household personal computers.

Even Americans who are well into their retirement years have adapted to the notion of researching local business services digitally.

About 90 percent of survey respondents felt that advertising in the Yellow Pages was ineffective.

While it's true that people often discover potential deathcare services through family connections or traditional word of mouth, that's far less the case as we progress further into the 21st century.

Our population has become increasingly transient. A half-century ago, many people still lived their entire lives in the same town. That's far rarer today.

Instead, many go straight to Google (or, less often, Yahoo or Bing) and do a search. It's free and convenient — the internet is at our fingertips 24 hours a day — so why not?

You can think of the evolution from print marketing to internet marketing as having a physical business that for many years was situated along a major road through your town.

Let's say that for many years, people saw your cemetery's physical location and inquired about services because they couldn't miss you.

Let's extend the hypothetical situation: A major U.S. highway is built in your town, just a few blocks from your business. Suddenly all the traffic comes down *that* highway, not the formerly major street where your store still resides. No one travels past you anymore.

You might have a great cemetery, but *no one knows you're there.*

You might even be *much better* than your competitors now situated along the U.S. highway, but it doesn't matter, because your competitors are the cemeteries people *actually see.* They're convenient to access. They are *where the people are.*

Today, ***the internet is where the people are***. And you get their attention by having a website that's optimized to be found when people are looking for what you do, specifically in your local market.

You get their attention by having comprehensive listings for your cemetery on Google and other major internet sites.

You get their attention by promoting your business on Facebook, Twitter, and other social media sites. And yes, I realize that might sound strange for a cemetery, but I assure you that there are tasteful ways to promote the important work you do. It has to be done thoughtfully, of course, but it can be done.

That might all sound like a lot, but it really isn't. If you need a hand with the technical issues, qualified internet marketing experts can handle those matters, letting you focus on what you do well: providing exceptional funeral services to families.

The key is to understand that in 2021, online marketing is no longer just a *facet* of your marketing plan.

It is the foundation of your marketing plan.

Business owners who ignore this fact will find themselves being ignored as we continue into this digital age.

In the rest of this book, I'll go over the basics. I'll explain how an online marketing professional can help you present your services to potential clientele and ensure excellent word of mouth for referrals.

I'll show you how a range of tools — many of them quite simple and affordable — can expand the reach of your business exponentially.

No matter what, the key thing I hope you'll understand is that in 2021, every month that goes by without actively promoting your cemetery online is a massive waste of potential. The playing field keeps changing all the time, and it's incredibly easy to get left behind.

The good news is this: If you act soon and get your "online house" in order, you won't just be benefitting from everything that a well-designed internet marketing campaign can do for you.

You'll also have a massive advantage on local competitors who have been slow to adapt to the new online marketing world. In this way, you can use the conventional wisdom of the deathcare industry to your benefit.

You will be recording in digital while they're still recording in analog. You'll be transmitting in high-definition while they're still using rabbit ears. You'll be operating in the present while they're still operating in the past. And that's a *gigantic* advantage in today's business world.

You want to be the cemetery holding that advantage, not the one watching from the sidelines.

I'm here to show you how to do it.

Section 1:

Lead Generation

CHAPTER 1
Search Engine Marketing (SEM)

If your cemetery has a website, it's a fair bet you have at least some idea of what **search engine marketing** (SEM) entails.

If it *doesn't* have a website, that problem needs to be rectified immediately. Having a website is a bare minimum requirement for a business in the 21st century, and it has been for some time. That's as true for burial and cremation services as it is for any business in the world.

Without a website, you might as well not have a front door or a phone. It's absolutely integral.

But I have to presume that in 2021, you at least have a website. (If you didn't, let's be honest, you wouldn't be reading this book.)

Regardless, let's go over the basics of SEM. In a nutshell, it's an umbrella term for a variety of tools that provide your site the *best possible visibility* online given certain factors.

In other words, you're obviously not competing for visibility against every other site in the world. No matter what you do, you're not going to be more visible than Amazon for retail goods or more visible than iTunes more music sales.

In SEM, you want your site to be more visible than the sites of local competitors. As a local business, that means optimizing your site (and your marketing efforts) to rank higher in search engine results pages (SERPs) than other cemetery providers in your market and in outlying areas you serve.

These days, online search is extremely specialized. There are strategies and tools that let you put your best foot forward in a particular area and market.

Some of these tools essentially require no advertising dollars; by optimizing your site with particular keywords and types of content, the site will organically rank well in your market and area.

Other tools require dipping into your marketing budget, such as letting you bid on particular keywords that people who are looking for your type of service will be using when they search.

For your business, this likely would include various forms of keyword phrases including targeted keywords that should include your city and state, along with the words *cemetery, burial, cremation, scattering garden, funeral prearrangement*, etc. The keywords you employ should specifically fit your particular business.

A successful internet marketing plan typically combines both approaches, one that balances the initiatives of organic SEO and paid advertising.

In this chapter, I'll cover the basics of **pay-per-click advertising** (PPC), **local search optimization**, and **search engine optimization** (SEO).

Pay-Per-Click Advertising (PPC)

Pay-per-click (PPC) is an umbrella term for several types of advertising, such as sponsored listings, paid search, partner ads, or sponsored links — with one thing in common:

In each type, you pay for the ad only when a user clicks it and is forwarded to your website (or whatever destination page you set up).

Most often, you'll find PPC ads atop pages when you do online searches — you'll recall those pages are called SERPs, or search engine results pages.

Google remains the dominating industry leader in search, with about *92 percent* of the organic search market share as of early 2021. It also comprises almost 30 percent of all digital ad spending globally. (Yes, it's *that* dominant.)

Its PPC function is an aspect of Google Ads, the venture that provides Google the vast majority of its revenue.

One of the coolest things about PPC ads is that they don't appear until someone completes a search.

Because they're dynamic, the ads that appear following the search will be relevant to whatever the user is searching for. The ads are, by definition, *targeting an interested party*.

The other obvious benefit is that the ad doesn't cost you a penny simply for appearing: ***You only pay when it gets clicked***, sending the user to your page and providing an opportunity to convert the visitor into a client.

Creating a PPC account can differ slightly depending on the platform (an internet marketing professional can explain the process and handle it for you). But here's the general game plan:

First, you'll create a PPC account with the particular platform, a simple enough process. Next, you'll create campaigns and ad groups.

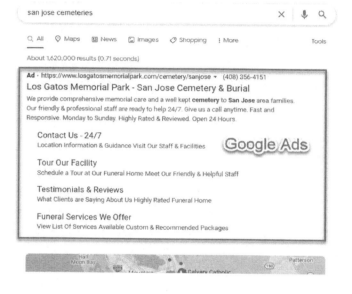

The campaign part is where you determine options such as the geography of the market you wish to reach. Because your cemetery relies on local customers, for example, you'll obviously want to target local people.

That's how localized search and advertising is these days: You can set it up so only people in your city, county, or state (depending on your preferences) see your ads and thus click on them.

The ad groups comprise your advertisements and keyword lists. An internet marketing professional can help you determine whether there are any other specific terms people will be searching for when they want to find a business that provides your particular services.

Remember that despite the name, *a keyword isn't necessarily just a single word*; it's very often a phrase. When a keyword phrase comprises more than one word (typically three or more), it's commonly called a **long-tail keyword**. You'll incorporate these keywords in the ads you run in your campaign.

The particular search engine for that campaign will determine how well the advertiser's campaigns and keywords match the user's particular search, and it will display the ads if there's a close match.

A few other factors determine whether your ad will show up. Every search engine has an algorithm that considers these factors and employs them with each search. These factors include:

- How closely do the keywords in the list match the actual search?
- Does the advertisement itself include a mention of what the user is looking for?
- Does the ad forward the user to a landing page selling the service the user wants?

- How much are you willing to pay for a user searching for these terms to see your ad (and hopefully click through to it)?

The final point — the actual amount of your bid — determines not only how much you'll pay, but also *how prominently* your ad is displayed on the page.

The specifics of each search engine's algorithm are not made public for a sound reason: It keeps less legitimate advertisers from gaming the system, crafting ads that exist only to get clicks without actually providing the user anything useful.

Google, in particular, has tweaked its algorithms substantially over the years to reward websites and advertisers who are legitimately providing good information and selling useful services and products. This is happening not only in PPC but in search engine rankings; we'll talk about this some more later.

The thing to remember is this: If you provide good content on your website/landing page and craft good PPC ads to market your cemetery, you'll be rewarded.

If your sites and ads are intended to mislead people into clicking through just to increase site traffic, you're taking a chance on being penalized by search providers, particularly Google.

This is one of the most common **black-hat** tactics. Anything you see referred to as "black hat" is a nefarious attempt to game the system. I can assure you that you never want to employ black-hat tactics. No truly reputable marketing company ever does.

If Google or other search engines catch you trying to game the system, your entire digital presence could be massively penalized. It's absolutely not worth the risk.

Instead, only work with companies who employ **white-hat** techniques. As you've surely inferred, that means doing things the right way. (Which we would hope every deathcare business would do.)

Whatever short-term benefits a business might receive from black-hat tactics will be far outweighed by the massive damage it can do when Google sniffs it out. And Google *will* sniff it out: It's like the IRS, just much faster and smarter.

Whether PPC is a valuable investment for your cemetery depends on several considerations. A big one is whether your website/landing page typically shows up near the top of the results when people are searching for the interment services you provide in your area.

As anyone can tell you, many people don't bother searching past the first page of SERPs. (Think about it: How often do you continue to Page 2 or 3 after doing a Google search?)

Being ranked on that first page is critical. If your cemetery isn't ranked there, for whatever reason — perhaps your site isn't sufficiently optimized for search engines, or you're in a highly competitive market — you're virtually invisible even if you're near the top of the listings on Page 2.

If you're even deeper in the SERPs, you're essentially *invisible*. Most searchers, if they don't find what they're looking for by Page 2, will just try a new search with some different keywords.

A PPC ad lets you essentially jump ahead of the SERP organic listings, putting your site/landing page right out front. Granted, this comes at a price, and some searchers can be reluctant to click on an ad as opposed to a search result per se.

However, PPC remains an *extremely effective tool* for many reasons. It provides a lot of control and is highly customizable. You only pay if the ad is clicked.

PPC also makes it easy to get extremely accurate statistics on whether your ad is effective, unlike most traditional types of advertising.

Best of all, if your cemetery needs to *rapidly increase its interment numbers*, PPC is the perfect tool for the job. PPC ads are highly visible, and they're especially well displayed on mobile devices.

Smartphone users can call your firm with a single click on a mobile PPC ad. And that's one of the biggest keys to digital marketing success: *Make it easy for a potential client to contact you.*

Whether you or a competitor gets the interment sometimes comes down to simply which one put up fewer obstacles for the searcher. When you make it easy, you get the call.

The analytics of PPC ads let you know which keywords people used to find your page, so you can tweak your keywords depending on which ones worked well (or poorly).

You'll know how many people departed a page on your site immediately after reaching it (known in the industry as your **bounce rate**) — and how many stuck around.

One of the biggest benefits of PPC (aka paid search) advertising is that it *bridges the time gap* between SEO improvements to your website and when they're recognized by Google.

Improving your organic SEO (the right way) goes a long way toward elevating your search rankings for people searching for deathcare services in your area.

However, Google only "crawls" your site (more on that later) occasionally, so it won't know immediately that you should be ranked high on the first page of results.

By comparison, PPC ads post almost immediately, letting you get your name right out front while you're waiting on Google to review your site and increase your organic ranking.

Some other benefits to PPC advertising to hone in on the right demographics and target the best leads:

Geography: This is a key factor in ensuring that you're targeting the most qualified leads. Analytical information lets you tweak the geography of your ads to concentrate on markets where they're doing well (and lets you pull them from markets where you're not garnering interest).

Similarly, one of the most useful aspects of PPC advertising is that you can target potential cemetery customers in very specific geographic areas.

For example, a PPC ad can be set to only appear *within a set radius* of a business's physical location. This is a great option for a cemetery, because local families almost always choose a local provider.

In addition to radius, PPC ads can be set to run only in particular ZIP codes or cities. Whatever exact areas you wish to target, your PPC ads can be focused entirely on them.

If you wish to cast a broader net, no problem. Unlike physical media such as the Yellow Pages, it costs *nothing extra* to target multiple cities.

You're not paying five or six times as much to run an ad in five or six cities —*one price fits all*. Thus the cost per lead is far less expensive than it would be with traditional media.

Day parting: As with geographical targeting, PPC ads can be set up to run only during the times of the day or week you want them to run.

Traditional service/product businesses most often stick with running ads during their operating hours (or perhaps extended to an hour or so before opening), but there's certainly a competitive advantage for a cemetery to run PPC ads even during nontraditional hours.

Day	Time period	Midnight	4:00 AM	8:00 AM	Noon	4:00 PM	8:00 PM
Monday	07:00 AM - 07:00 PM						
Tuesday	07:00 AM - 05:30 PM						
Wednesday	Running all day						
Thursday	Running all day						
Friday	Noon - 04:00 PM						
Saturday	Running all day						
Sunday	Running all day						

Controlling lead flow: The scheduling of PPC ads can be easily modified to increase traffic. Google charges based on a daily budget.

Let's say you typically spend $30 per day, but there's a period where you need to increase your new business flow and have some room in your budget. You can increase it to $50 for more coverage.

On the other hand, let's say your cemetery is already very busy. You could knock down your PPC ad budget to $15 for a while to save some money. (If you're busy already, why spend money on ads?)

And if you're literally *overwhelmed* with business at a particular time — a good problem to have, but a challenge nonetheless — you can even *pause your ads* for whatever time frame you determine.

In this sense, running PPC ads is like turning the knob on a faucet: You can open it up to flow freely, turn it down to a trickle, or turn it off entirely for a while, all dependent on your needs at the time.

Instant traffic: As I noted before, PPC ads let you be seen on the first page of search results almost immediately. *You're paying for the opportunity to jump to the front of the pack.*

This makes PPC a powerful tool for seeing a very fast return on an online marketing campaign. When used in tandem with organic SEO and local optimization strategies, you will see your traffic soar and watch it continue climbing in both the short and long term.

PPC ads are never static: Anything can be tweaked, adjusted, or swapped out at any time. With print media, you're stuck with the same print ad for a long time. In the case of the Yellow Pages, you're stuck with it for an *entire year*.

If there are changes in your business — e.g., you add a new memorial garden or columbarium, you expand the geographical area you're targeting, you revise your services in some way — the Yellow Pages ad will still have all the old information until it's time for a new edition of the print directory.

PPC ads let you change the content on the fly. If you want to make a change for a short time to increase business, such reducing prices or a special discount on family or companion plots, you can have the new ad appearing "live" to searchers in only a day or two.

Trying lots of variations: With a typical print ad, you come up with terms and phrasing you think will work best, cross your fingers, and hope it does the job.

PPC advertising lets you try out many different variations of ads catered to the keywords you want. You literally could have hundreds or even thousands of different variations employed at the same time.

(To keep things easy to manage, you'll likely only want to employ a handful of keywords, but you get the idea.)

This also allows for **split testing** of the different choices, letting you know quickly which ads have the most impact and which are less successful.

Additionally, when you have several ads running simultaneously with differently worded long-tail keywords, the ads people see will typically match up with the terms they're specifically searching for.

If they search for "cemetery services," they'll get the ad with *that* focus. If they search for "spreading ashes" (it's less likely the layperson will use the technical term "cremated remains"), they'll get the ad with *that* focus. Same with "veteran burial" or "local cemeteries" or "green burial," etc.

This is another way in which PPC advertising beats out print, because in something such as the Yellow Pages, you have to determine which sections you want to be listed in and place ads in *all* of them.

Excellent branding tool: If improving brand awareness is a critical concern for your cemetery, PPC is an effective tool. If people click on your ad, that's great: They're coming to your website to consider your location and services. If they don't, you're *still getting exposure* to lots of people searching for what you provide, improving brand awareness.

Note: Now, I know that terms such as "brand awareness" can sound a bit too "business-oriented" to many cemetery owners. You're not a *brand*, you're a cemetery, right?

Well…not entirely.

You actually are a brand.

After all, if you're that good at helping families in your area, aren't you helping *them* out by ensuring they can easily find you and work with you? Are they well served by working with a competing cemetery that doesn't serve them as well as you do?

You're a brand now. Accept it and incorporate it into your marketing strategy.

You don't necessarily have to pay for the top spot in PPC ads: Consider the NFL draft. Teams regularly trade down from their initial spots in the draft because the value isn't there for the player they need in a particular position.

They often can obtain that player even when they pick a little further down in the draft — and ultimately *pay less money* for the player, because the spot where a player is picked goes a long way toward determining his salary.

(In the draft, teams also can get more draft picks for trading away a high pick, but that part's not relevant here.)

The same is true of PPC advertising. For some industries, and this includes cemeteries, bidding for the top spot can cost a lot more than the value it delivers. The top spot for a particular keyword is much more expensive than, let's say, the fourth spot.

Having that top spot makes sense for a business for which people will likely not take the time to perform any additional research — for example, a locksmith or a bail bonds provider. For those types of businesses, people often click on the very first ad that pops up when it's an emergency or time is of the essence.

In that sense, getting a higher position might be worth the investment for your business. If it's critical for your business to be the *very first option* families see when dealing with an unexpected death, it's worth paying the extra freight for that top spot.

However, when it comes to services that tend to be researched more extensively (because time is not of the essence), there's less benefit to paying for the top spot. In that case, an interested party likely will be checking out several providers that pop up for those keywords.

In that situation, ranking third or fourth is just as good as ranking first, and it's substantially less expensive.

PPC also can include display ads: While the focus of this discussion has been PPC ads that appear on search engine results pages, you can also publish display ads on the pages of Google's display ad partners. These are the types of ads you commonly see on larger websites.

In general, advertising for SERPs is intended for to attract customers who are looking to purchase services immediately. Display ads on larger websites are more intended for branding and to attract people who might be interested in your services down the line — so that's best for preplanning.

The process for publishing display ads on Google is known as the Google Display Network. Google has "flexible reach" targeting, which ensures greater control over targeting and the ability to try out different targeting combinations more easily.

Remarketing: This also falls under the preplanning umbrella, and it is another great benefit of PPC advertising.

When you employ Google Ads, you also can elect remarketing, which means that your ads will continue to make a case for your cemetery with people who have shown an interest in your services by visiting your site previously.

Google can track who has visited your site and continue to display your ads for these leads when they visit other sites. This lets you reengage with leads who did not purchase immediately.

You can even customize the messaging in this ad to make a special offer that will compel them to return to your site and do business with you.

Remarketing has shown to be hugely successful in recent years across a wide variety of industries. It's a marketing strategy that works very well to attract people who are planning ahead for deathcare services.

An important consideration in remarketing is that you want to set the ads to run only for a particular time frame or to appear only a certain number of times. That way, remarketing targets won't feel like they're being "stalked" by your ads all over the internet. No one wants that, and it would be bad for your firm's reputation.

Thus, remarketing must be employed surgically, and a good marketing firm can help you with figuring out the proper time frames and/or number of appearances.

Summary of PPC advantages

Virtually instant traffic to your advertisements
- You can have ads on the front pages of Google (and/or Bing and Yahoo, if desired) in just few hours.

A world of options print Yellow Pages can't provide
- Use text-based ads, streaming video ads, banner ads, and more.
- Advertise to a targeted audience in minutes.
- Be rewarded for creating good ads with lower ad costs.

Laser targeting
- Advertise to people who are looking *right now* for the services you offer.
- Quickly test to determine which ads bring you qualified traffic.
- Easily monitor which keywords attract visitors who actually convert into customers and which do not, letting you easily alter your ad to include the highest-converting keywords.

Local/regional targeting
- Target users by location, allowing you to specifically reach local customers.
- You can choose where and when you want your ads to be visible.

Cost-effectiveness
- Pay only when a customer clicks on your ad.
- Benefit from free branding even when people don't click on your ad.
- Determine your costs based on your own objectives: Specify exactly how much you want to spend, and even set a maximum daily and/or monthly budget.

Powerful money-making tool
- If you could spend one dollar to make two dollars, how many dollars would you spend?

That's how a well-optimized PPC campaign works.

Measurable results
- You get real-time ROI data through conversion tracking data.
- Every aspect of the process is trackable.
- Google collects and analyzes all key data for you and will auto-send you reports.

Summary of PPC disadvantages

- Only through paying the advertising cost will you be able to determine the ROI of various ads.
- Each new visitor costs money: While you could get some return visitors who bookmark your site, in general when you stop paying, the visitors stop coming.
- Having your ads link to a high-converting site is a must: A good PPC campaign can drive lots of targeted traffic to your site, but if that site doesn't turn visitors into clientele, it's wasted money.

A note on the landing page

With all that said, a PPC ad campaign is *only as good as the landing page it's selling*.

Let's say you're looking for a home and you drive past a gorgeous billboard advertising an amazing condominium complex just a mile away.

It's advertising resort living at a fraction of the price, tons of amenities, and a great neighborhood. It sounds like paradise

So you head over to the address, full of excitement and glee, and when you arrive, you discover... it's a dump.

It looks like it hasn't been renovated in 100 years, it has a rusty, broken gate out front, and the parking lot is covered in trash that's clearly been piling up for weeks.

Are you going to bother driving onto the property and checking it out? Or are you going to get out of there as fast as you can before you get mugged?

That's what happens when a landing page doesn't deliver what the PPC ad promised.

If the landing page is poorly designed, or if the website isn't selling what the typical visitor would expect, the visitor is going to "click out" in a matter of seconds. And you just paid for a visit that did you no good.

I'll get into landing page and website optimization more in a bit, but it's critical to remember that there's no point to purchasing PPC ads if you're sending visitors somewhere they don't want to be.

Anything from a lack of relevant content to slow page loads can prompt a visitor to set sail in a matter of seconds.

I'll get into website conversions elsewhere in this book, but the bottom line is this: Your PPC ads are only as effective as your website is. Your SEO efforts are only as effective as your website is. Your offline advertising... well, you get the idea.

Just as there would be no point to spending thousands on marketing a pizza parlor with terrible food, health department citations, and a lazy waitstaff, there's no point to driving families to a cemetery website that has poor navigation, no obvious call to action, and little information on the firm and its services.

The pizza parlor needs to focus *first* on cleaning up the kitchen, improving its food, and hiring better servers. The cemetery site must focus *first* on better serving its visitors and converting them into clientele. Only then will PPC ads and other marketing methods generate revenue.

A site can attract tons of traffic, but if those visitors don't turn into clientele, the traffic is pointless. Once you've transformed your cemetery site into a conversion-generating machine, PPC ads will work wonders.

<u>Local Search Optimization</u>

In the most basic sense, when we're talking about local search (you'll sometimes see this capitalized as Local Search, but I'll stay old-school here), we're simply referring to online searches that have a geographical component. (In the deathcare industry, of course, services tend to be extremely localized.)

If you live in St. Petersburg, Florida, and you need to have a replacement odometer installed (by a trained mechanic) for your 2012 Buick LaCrosse, you typically won't simply search for "2012 Buick LaCrosse odometer" or "Buick LaCrosse mechanic" or "2012 Buick LaCrosse repair."

You'll usually add something that *includes your actual location*. So you'll add "St. Petersburg" to your search terms.

(If you're searching in English, you'll far more likely get results for Florida's St. Petersburg than the Russian city, but depending on what the results are, you might need to add Florida.)

Of course, St. Petersburg is also part of the Tampa Bay metropolitan area, with both Tampa and Clearwater each just a short drive away. So you might want to expand your search to Tampa Bay or to each of those particular cities.

But with all of that said... on most devices, the search engine will *already know where you are* and automatically deliver local results, even if you don't add a location. This is usually true as well if you include "near me" in the search.

In recent years, search has become increasingly local. Again, this owes a lot to the massive expansion of affordable mobile technology. Smartphones and tablets (and more recently, even *smartwatches*) let people navigate their neighborhoods easily.

As of January 2021, Google reported that *46 percent* of searches have local intent. For comparison, consider that when I wrote my first book on deathcare six years ago, that number was only 20 percent.

Additionally, according to a fall 2020 survey, 91 percent of searchers who researched a local business on Google continued the process by *calling a local business within 24 hours*.

It's actually rather ironic: In its early days, the internet let us quickly and easily interact with people and places all around the world. These days, we're more likely to use it to find places and services right in our hometowns. (This effect was also amplified by COVID lockdowns and restrictions in 2020 and early 2021.)

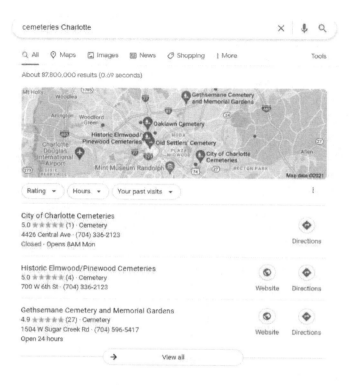

It's actually rather ironic: In its early days, the internet let us quickly and easily interact with people and places all around the world. These days, we're more likely to use it to find places and services right in our hometowns. (This effect was also amplified by COVID lockdowns and restrictions in 2020 and early 2021.)

Of course, that's why local search optimization is so critical for cemeteries in 2021 and beyond. As I noted in the introduction, this is how people will find your business these days.

Some might open up the Yellow Pages if they have that book lying around the house. But many will search on their PC, or tablet, or smartphone.

Optimizing your business for local search ensures not only that you're putting your best foot forward for potential clients — it ensures that you *show up at all*. You need to do this to show up on Google Maps, the most widely used graphical search provider in the world.

Practically every day, I find myself needing to know where something is near my location — an ATM, a gas station, a restaurant, a grocery store.

My phone automatically knows where I am, thanks to GPS. Businesses that are optimized for local search will pop up as soon as I search, and the listings show me how far away they are, directions, etc.

But that's not all: When a business has included its business hours on its **Google My Business** listing, I automatically know whether it's open or closed — or how long I have to get there until it *does* close. (I'll explain GMB more in a bit.)

I can also see ratings and reviews from customers, helping me know whether I can trust that particular mechanic, hair stylist, or retailer.

As I noted before, this is one of the key processes people now use to find local businesses. If you're not taking advantage of it — if your business isn't listed in Google, or if the information there is out of date or incomplete — you're placing yourself at a massive disadvantage compared to your competitors.

Getting to know Google My Business

It's useful to understand a little history here:

In the mid-2000s, Google had a few different names for its local business listing platforms. It started with Google Local, Google Maps, and the Google Local Business Center.

Over the next few years, well, it got confusing. Google Local and Google Maps merged, with the new combination briefly taking the name Google Local and then switching to Google Maps.

A few years later, the company launched "Google Place Pages for Google Maps." A little later (June 2011), we finally saw the arrival of Google+, which Google intended to be a true rival to social platforms such as Twitter and Facebook.

In its wake, virtually everything became Google+ branded. We got Google+ Pages, Google+ Your Business, Google+ Brand, Google+ Local...

Anyway, we'll cut to the chase. Google+ (the social platform) was virtually dead on arrival, although Google kept trying to make it a thing for several more years. It finally gave up in 2018. As you read this, Google+ is relegated to the dustbin of history.

Instead, we have Google My Business, which is essentially one-stop shopping for everything that used to fall under the umbrella of Google+ Local, Google+ Your Business, Google+ Places, etc.

GMB itself actually has been around several years now, but it's become more firmly entrenched as "*the*

Google tool for small business" in recent years as Google has clarified its suite of tools.

A few reasons why I broke down that history for you:
1) You need to remember that as great as Google is at many things, it also initiates a lot of tools that fail and/or end up being reworked or renamed. That's the nature of such a creative industry.
2) The digital marketing landscape changes all the time. To be competitive, you need to stay current — or at least hire a marketing company that stays current *for you* and is constantly evolving along with the changes.
3) Regardless of all the rebranding of Google's tools, it is *completely dedicated* to helping small businesses market themselves online. And that all starts with Google My Business.

As you probably already know, yes, people actually do review cemeteries and providers of related deathcare services on Yelp and other review sites. Having the strongest reputation in your area immediately makes you a frontrunner for these services.

Surveys show that 74 percent of consumers consider online reviews as trustworthy as personal recommendations, which is why ensuring you have positive (and preferably exceptionally positive) reviews on your GMB listing is so important.

When dealing with businesses in other industries, this is where I typically would note that it's a good idea to ask satisfied customers to review your business positively.

At RRM, we also utilize a proprietary email program that solicits reviews from families in a very thoughtful, understanding manner (after a proper waiting period following services).

Asking for reviews is also certainly a consideration when providing prearrangement sales. If you're providing great customer service for individuals in the process, they'll be receptive to reviewing their interactions with you positively.

(I cover reputation and reviews in more depth in a later chapter, so look for more details there.)

Your GMB listing also effectively acts as a blog, thanks to the Google Posts feature. You can provide updates and reach out to customers, providing useful information and showing potential customers you're highly engaged and communicative.

Publishing short updates on Google Posts also helps with your website SEO (because Google sees you more as an influencer in your industry), so you're getting two benefits every time you post!

Gethsemane Cemetery and Memorial Gardens

Website Directions Save Call

4.9 ★★★★★ 27 Google reviews
Cemetery in Charlotte, North Carolina

Address: 1504 W Sugar Creek Rd, Charlotte, NC 28262

Hours: Open 24 hours

Phone: (704) 596-5417

Suggest an edit · Own this business?

Know this place? Share the latest info

Products   View all

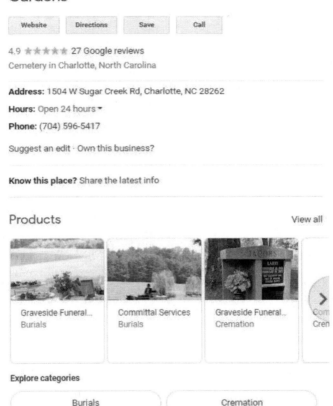

Graveside Funeral... Burials

Committal Services Burials

Graveside Funeral... Cremation

Explore categories

Burials   Cremation

Don't forget Bing Places for Business

Of course, Bing has its own local option, and while it makes sense to make Google My Business your top priority, that doesn't mean you should entirely ignore Bing.

While Bing comprises a comparatively tiny portion of the search market — speaking of great branding, there's a reason you never hear someone say "just Bing it" instead of "just Google it" — Bing still plays a role.

And that's simply because Bing is Microsoft's search engine, and Microsoft remains an enormous player in computing, thanks to its popular Windows software.

That's why when you buy a new laptop or desktop computer with the Windows operating system, the default search engine (on Microsoft's default web browser, Microsoft Edge) is Bing.

Granted, most people with even a modest understanding of technology know they can change their computer's default web browser in just a couple of minutes. (It's incredibly easy.) So if they prefer a browser such as Google Chrome to Microsoft Edge, as many do, they just make the change.

(Note: As of May 2021, Chrome had over **64 percent** of the web browser market share, compared to just over **less than 4 percent** for Microsoft Edge.)

Additionally, virtually all smartphone users in the United States either use Android devices (Android is a Google operating system) or iPhones (Apple). As of

April 2021, the market was split essentially right down the middle: about 51 percent of people used Android phones, while about 48 percent used iPhones.

(That's actually a big increase for Android, which only owned about 43 percent compared to iPhone's 56 percent just three years earlier.)

The other operating systems *combined* comprised a fraction of 1 percent. So Android and iPhone truly are the only contemporary players in the market.

Regardless, there's no reason not to ensure your cemetery is properly listed on Bing Places for Business (previously known as Bing Local).

Your cemetery has a physical address, so it likely already has a Bing Places for Business listing; you simply have to claim it.

Much like Google My Business, you'll want to ensure your profile is completed with all the pertinent information for your cemetery.

Note that if you haven't filled out your Bing Places for Business listing previously, you might have an even more convenient option. Bing actually lets you *import* the information from your GMB account, if you wish. (This won't affect your GMB listing.) It's right there in the setup process.

Just make sure that you've checked all the information in your Bing listing after the import. Don't just assume it's all correct.

Unlike GMB, Bing Places for Business doesn't have its own native reviews.

For many years, it partnered with Yelp (as with Yahoo, we're going to leave off the exclamation point for simplicity), one of the most popular online review services.

However, over the past couple of years, it's regularly incorporated TripAdvisor and Facebook reviews as well. Any combination of these can appear on your Bing Places for Business page.

There are some other differences between these two platforms, and it's useful to note that Yahoo has a local platform of its own, but most of the points noted earlier about Google My Business relate to all the services.

The most important takeaway is that completing all your business's information on these platforms — and ensuring it's accurate and kept up to date — is necessary for putting your best foot forward when people are searching for local businesses. These services are built to accommodate mobile users, a segment that has grown massively just in the past couple of years.

Citations

Another very important aspect of local search optimization is the use of **citations**. These are mentions of your cemetery that appear on the internet regardless of whether there's an actual link to your website.

To superpower your local SEO, you must generate a substantial number of local citations.

A local citation could occur when your cemetery is noted in general text in an online listing of businesses in your local market or your region. It could be a mention in a news story, white paper, or trend piece.

Although these references to your business don't include a direct link, they are key components in the ranking algorithms of Google and other top search engines.

The more you're referenced on other sites, especially if they're among the more regularly visited and indexed sites, the more "useful" the search engines think your business is. This improves the rankings of your business's website.

A citation on something such as a chamber of commerce or county business index is especially useful. This is also true of a citation in a major newspaper or other news site.

That's because these citations lend even more legitimacy and credibility to your site — it's awfully hard to "fake" an appearance in a major newspaper, so the search engine knows you're an actual operating business.

A good internet marketing specialist can help you learn how to improve your citations, but in general, the key is to ensure you're properly listed in all legitimate listing services that are appropriate for your cemetery.

Be sure you're included in local blogs, locally focused directories, and directories/blogs that are specific to cemeteries.

Of course, if your cemetery specifically caters to a particular religious, cultural, or demographic segment (e.g., Catholic, Jewish, military, African-American,

Latinx, etc.), you absolutely want to leverage citation opportunities in related blogs and directories too.

If you are involved with something newsworthy that can get your business named in a newspaper story or on a local television station's website — such as providing free funeral services for a decorated veteran or a cherished member of the community — that's a great citation to have.

Quick tip: Doing community service such as this is a spectacular way to get publicity, because the local news rarely covers such businesses (excepting paid advertising) outside of brief listings, and news stories are the types of citations Google and other search engines will prioritize.

And frankly, community interaction is a great way to differentiate your business from the stigma many Americans hold in their limited views about cemeteries. Take advantage of the opportunity to show that you're not a "spooky place" but a wonderful final resting place for people who lived great lives in your community.

Local search advantages

- It's free, which allows for infinite return on investment.
- It lets families rate and review your cemetery, so if you're good at what you do, you'll stand out from the crowd.

- It adds your site to Google Maps, one of the top ways people discover local businesses now
- It lets you add specific keywords to your business description, giving you a leg up on competitors who have not done this.

Local search disadvantages

- A limited number of businesses automatically show up as a search result.
- It can take greater than a month to show up in the listings, and the likelihood of appearing high in the results (or in the first seven at all) depends on optimization.
- You can only optimize your business for the five to ten most relevant keywords.

Search Engine Optimization (SEO)

An entire book can be written about search engine optimization (SEO). In fact, many have been, and many more will be. There are many facets to SEO, and the best practices are regularly changing. Frankly, they've changed substantially just in the six years since the first book I wrote about deathcare marketing.

Here, I'll touch on the highlights.

You undoubtedly know the purpose of SEO: It's a set of processes intended to help ensure your website/landing page ranks as highly as possible in search results.

Ever since search engines began appearing on the internet, website owners and webmasters have understood the power of ranking as highly as possible on SERPs.

It's not exactly a new concept: Everything else being equal, you're more likely to get people's business if *yours is the first option they see.*

That's why print magazines (yes, a few still exist in 2021) want to be at the *front* of the racks in physical bookstores (if you can still find one of those today — it's not easy).

That's why businesses for many years would select names that put them at the front of white pages and Yellow Pages listings:

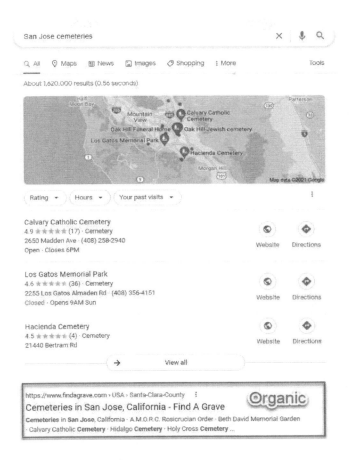

Ace Plumbing was upstaged by Abacus Plumbing, which was eclipsed by Aardvark Plumbing, then A Aardvark Plumbing, followed by A AA Aardvark Plumbing... I'm sure you remember how that went. You'll still see a lot of local businesses today using this tricky naming process.

Today, however, alphabetization doesn't matter much. Search engines don't care whether your business name starts with an A or Z. They take no notice of whether you have a really colorful name or a bland one — that's not part of the equation.

Granted, your business's name *does* matter, but only in the sense that the SEO will be improved if *terms in the name are highly relevant* to what people will be searching for.

That is, if instead of handling funeral services, you happened to sell custom hubcaps in Charlotte, naming your business Charlotte Custom Hubcaps (and snagging that as a domain name as well) would be a big help for your SEO.

If you're a cemetery in Tucson, obviously, something like "Tucson Cemetery" makes things easiest for search engines and potential leads.

But before we dig into how SEO works, let's start off by defining a few terms:

White-hat SEO vs. black-hat SEO: I touched on these terms earlier, but here's a little more context.

As soon as webmasters realized that search engines were using certain elements of websites to determine how highly those sites should rank, some started to think of ways to game the system.

When a site is using tricks intended only to improve rankings or traffic without providing an equivalent benefit to actual visitors, that's *black-hat SEO*.

On the other hand, when a site uses techniques that improve rankings and traffic that are integral to providing a benefit for visitors, that's *white-hat SEO*.

Sneaky sites (and their sneaky webmasters) benefited from black-hat SEO for many years, but those days are largely over now. Search engines (particularly Google) tweaked their algorithms substantially to punish sites that used black-hat tactics and reward ones that followed a white-hat approach.

As I noted earlier, it's *absolutely not worth it* to work with a firm that promises big results through black-hat practices, no matter how cheap the price.

The money you save up front by working with these con artists — and that's truly what they are — won't come close to making up for the business you lose when Google banishes your cemetery site to page eight of its SERPS.

In extreme cases, Google can even *ban your URL altogether*. And once you're on Google's bad side, you're in serious trouble: Google has a very long memory.

Spiders/crawling: With rare exception, search engines don't employ people to actually visit websites and determine whether those sites are relevant and useful (and thus worthy of being ranked highly). Instead, they create software known as **spiders**. These spiders go to websites and then read and index the information there, a process known as **crawling** the site.

They don't just review the content visitors can see, but also information in the coding of the site. The info they collect is then factored into complicated algorithms that determine how highly a site should be ranked for various searches people do online.

Organic search results: Otherwise known as natural search results, these are the basic unpaid search results — as opposed to paid listings, "sponsored" listings, or ads — people get when they search for keywords.

As you've surely noticed, searching for anything on Google these days will result in a page of SERPs that include both organic and paid results, and sometimes it can be tricky to tell the difference.

Ultimately, your cemetery services website or has two very distinct objectives.

One objective is to put your best foot forward for actual human visitors. You want people who visit your site to be impressed by your business and want to do work with you.

Your goal is to create *conversions*, which essentially means that the site prompts the visitor to take an action toward becoming a client.

Most often, you'll want the visitor to either call you, email you, or fill out an online form for more information on planning or purchasing an interment option. If the visitor takes any of these actions, you could consider that a conversion.

(Of course, that doesn't necessarily mean the visitor ultimately will contract with you. That will be up to your salesperson and how well he or she succeeds at closing the sale. However, as long as your website prompted one of the actions noted above, the site properly *converted* the visitor.)

To this end, you want the content on your site to read well, provide useful information, and sell the visitor on the fact that you provide the best interment option compared to any local competitors.

Beyond dealing with human visitors, the other objective of your website is to sell the relevance of your site to the search engine spiders.

This is where SEO strategies come into play. By employing these strategies in the site's content, design, and coding, you can persuade these spiders to rank your site highly when people search for keywords that would be naturally associated with burials, urns, plots, cremation, and associated services and products.

As you might expect, one of the greatest concerns Google and other search providers have is that sites try to game the system to make the *spiders* happy without making actual human *visitors* happy.

This is why Google, in particular, has started heavily penalizing sites that use this approach. It wants the sites that rank highest to be the most useful for *actual people* who are actively searching for what you provide.

You might wonder why certain sites would game the system with pages that rank highly but provide nothing good for the visitors. People will just click out immediately when they realize there's nothing there for them, right?

Some site owners/webmasters (outside the funeral industry) do this because their business model simply pays them for *hits*: visits to sites, whether or not the visitors bounce out immediately.

These sites use advertising models where it doesn't matter at all whether the site itself is useful, just that they've recorded hits for advertisers to the site.

If a visitor goes on to click on an ad on the site, the site gets paid even more. Ultimately, these sites are not really selling anything or providing any service; they exist only to trick people into clicking through to the site.

These are the types of sites Google has penalized with tweaks to its algorithm. Google literally changes its search algorithm as many as *500 times* in a given year. Doing so ensures that people searching Google will find sites that provide the information and products they want.

This provides a great opportunity for legitimate business owners such as you. By combining high-quality content with legitimate white-hat SEO techniques, you make *both* your human visitors and search engine spiders happy.

When your written copy is relevant, easy to read, and compelling (not just stuffed with irrelevant keywords to trick the spiders into ranking you more highly), you'll actually be increasing your SEO and receiving higher rankings (and thus increased traffic).

It's a lot harder to game the system now, and that's not a bad thing at all: It means legitimate websites such as yours are rising to the top while the tricksters are relegated to the depths of the SERPs.

At the risk of belaboring this point, I need to be clear: Sites that use black-hat tactics are massively penalized when Google figures out what's happening. (And Google *always* finds out.)

They can plummet so deep in search rankings that no one will ever see them, and when the tricks used are particularly egregious, Google (and Bing, Yahoo, etc.) can even remove the site completely from search rankings.

If an internet marketing "expert" claims he or she can substantially improve your site's rankings or traffic without making substantial improvements to the actual content, design, and relevance of the site, don't walk away — *run*.

Trying to trick Google is a very, *very* bad idea. Instead, find a legitimate internet marketing pro with a great white-hat SEO record.

Great original content is great, but sham experts will rip off content from other sites and use it on yours. Relevant incoming and outgoing links are great, but these scammers will add links from hundreds of irrelevant websites.

They'll hook you into massive link exchange sites that provide nothing useful for your actual human visitors. The brief jump your site might see in rankings is not worth the damage that will occur when the hammer comes down.

Doing it the right way

So how do you do it the right way? It's important to understand what a search engine is looking for when determining how highly your site/landing page should rank in SERPs.

Though this relates to all major search engines, let's just use Google as an example. Every time someone does a search for certain keywords, Google's search engine considers the following:

Site authority: Is your site an authority on what the searcher is looking for? Having lots of high-quality, original content regarding the subject (in your case, information related to plots, urn gardens, general funeral material, etc.) signals that it is. So do incoming links from other legitimate sites Google considers authoritative on subjects such as burial, cremation, veteran death benefits, etc.

By filling your site with original content that informs and educates people on the respectful process of dealing with deathcare, you're signaling to Google that you're an authority on the industry — while simultaneously establishing *trustworthiness* with human visitors that you'll take good care of them and their loved ones.

Social media: I'll discuss social media in greater detail later in this book, but the more citations your site receives in social media, the more authoritative it appears on the subject.

Site performance: If your site receives lots of visitors, that's a big help. If those visitors not only stick around but also click on several other pages contained in the site, even better. Google tracks all these things, and they all affect your SEO.

You can view this as a cyclical process: The more visitors you get, the better your site will rank. The better your site ranks, the more visitors you get. So once you get that engine running, it virtually sustains itself. And your cemetery website keeps growing in authority and popularity.

Content: *This doesn't just mean the words on the site.* This also means images, videos, and other media relevant to what the searcher is looking for. The more *original* the content you populate your site with, the better.

I like to say that ***content is king***, and for good reason: More than anything these days, the quality of your content will determine how well (or how poorly) your site ranks.

I talk more about content elsewhere in this book, but the key thing to remember is that your site *absolutely needs good content*. There's no shortcut around this that will produce the SEO and conversions you need.

I realize that very few independent cemeteries have the in-house resources to generate lots of strong content itself, which means this is an area where you'll almost certainly need to contract out.

You can do so by either contracting directly with a qualified independent freelance writer or working with an experienced marketing company that has a team of solid writers.

The latter option typically works best, because you won't have to worry about all the administrative aspects of working with an individual contractor.

Site design: Sites that are well designed are not only most helpful to human visitors, but to spiders as well.

A well-designed site makes it easy for the spiders to interpret how relevant the site is to what people are looking for. A properly designed site also includes keywords in its image tags and coding to communicate relevance.

Page speed/page load times: I cover this issue in more depth in the website conversions chapter, but it's also very important for SEO, so allow me to preview a bit of that here.

American now expect pages on business websites to fully load in a matter of seconds. This is especially true for smartphone users, but it extends to people who view sites on tablets and desktop computers as well.

In summer 2018, Google started making the speed at which pages on your website a major ranking factor in search engine rankings, and it's even more so in 2021.

That simply means that the faster your site loads, the higher you'll rank in SERPs (against other cemeteries in your area). See the website conversions chapter for more on this topic.

As for how to employ all these techniques and practices, that's a subject for a book much more specific to SEO.

You can use such resources to learn more about determining what keywords to use in your copy and coding, designing your site for maximum impact on human visitors and spiders, and tracking how well your site is doing compared to your competitors. Regularly analyzing and tweaking your approach is *absolutely necessary*.

If, like most cemetery owners, you prefer to concentrate on running your business, a professional internet marketing professional can handle all those elements for you.

Just remember to find a provider who uses white-hat tactics and can provide great examples of having increased sites' rankings through the legitimate methods detailed here.

It's always most beneficial to work with a company that has experience with cemeteries and funeral homes, because messaging and other key aspects are very different from other business types.

You don't want to contract with an agency that markets you the same way it markets hair salons or sandwich shops, of course. Marketing a cemetery requires an understanding of nuance and thoughtfulness that's alien to most agencies.

Link building

As with SEO in general, link building is a broad subject. It's an essential part of SEO, because search engines still place a lot of importance on which sites your cemetery website links *to* (**outgoing links**) and which sites link to *you* (**incoming links**).

If your cemetery site is an island unto itself, that suggests to Google that your site is not very useful or influential, regardless of whether that's true.

That's why so much black-hat SEO is focused on artificially building up rankings based on link networks and purchased links. Not all link networks are necessarily "tricks," and not all purchased links are necessarily irrelevant, but they've been used so irresponsibly that it now requires great care to ensure you don't make Google think you're up to no good.

When you build links appropriately and organically, you're employing a powerful tool for your site. I'll go over a few of the basics here:

In essence, every live webpage in existence has the ability to "vote" for other webpages by linking to them. How many votes are provided by an incoming link depends on several factors, but a key one is the *SEO strength* of the site that's voting.

How much the votes from that incoming link affect your SEO also can depend on the *relevance of the linking website to yours*.

That's why getting inbound links from influential sites specifically related to deathcare is extremely useful for your cemetery website.

It's also important to consider **link velocity**, which refers to how quickly your site acquires new links. If your site gets hundreds or even thousands of new links in one fell swoop, that's far less beneficial than steadily aggregating links over a matter of time.

If your cemetery site suddenly gets lots of new links, that's a *huge red flag* for Google. If it steadily builds links over time, Google interprets that as a natural process for a site that's properly growing in influence.

The best way to get other sites to link to yours is to *create useful, interesting content* about deathcare. A blog that's specific to your main focus is thus incredibly beneficial for attracting links.

Post regularly with original copy that's relevant to sites you want to link to yours. Make sure the copy is clean and grammatically correct: No one wants to link to a site that reads like it was written by Yoda after a three-day bender.

Also, don't only write copy that specifically sounds like you're pitching your cemetery and its services. While it's fine to mention your business on occasion, you're far more likely to attract incoming links if you're providing solid information that's *useful for everyone.*

As I'll discuss further in the social media section, it's smart to blog about matters that are interesting to the AARP crowd, even if the subjects aren't specifically about funerals and burials.

You can talk about retirement, healthcare, caregiving, vacationing, financial planning, exercise for seniors, military issues, etc.

Your blog will generate a lot more readership and interest if it covers a broad spectrum of issues. (If it exclusively covered deathcare issues, some potential readers might consider it to morbid and/or depressing.)

Also, adding images, infographics and other types of content specific to the deathcare industry makes your blog more SEO-attractive.

Again, you'll probably have to contract out for content generation, unless you have someone on staff who's truly great at writing interesting, SEO-friendly copy (and whose time you can free up to work on it).

Other ways to encourage links:

- **Make it easy for people to bookmark your posts and forward them to friends.** Several tools let people do this with a single click. This is a great way to make posts go "viral" and gain links. (Remember, virtually any time of business — including a cemetery — can create interesting content people will want to share. Open your mind about all the subjects you can cover. Just make sure you don't get into any controversial territory.)

- **Include a link back to your website when you comment on other sites and blogs.** Most sites include a field for that, so use it. Obviously, be sure your comments are interesting and colorful, and that they represent your business in a professional manner. You never want a controversial comment — and *especially not a crude or profane comment* — linked to your business site. That's true of any business type, but obviously it's imperative in your line of work. If you delegate commenting you a staff member, make sure he or she knows to always communicate in a thoughtful manner.

- **Submit your site to directories.** There are many different directories — some free, some requiring a paid membership — that will be included as incoming links when you get listed with them. Obviously, be sure to list your site with directories that are specific to deathcare, along with your local chamber of commerce.

- **Link to other relevant sites whenever possible.** This refers to **reciprocal links**, which can be tricky. They aren't nearly as beneficial when they appear to search engines to simply be a one-for-one trade. (It's exactly like "I'll follow you if you follow me back" on Twitter.) However, in general, outgoing links help SEO when you're linking to quality sites, and sometimes those sites will link to you down the line. This will not hurt your SEO. Think of it as karma. Like the Beatles said, "the love you get is equal to the love you give."

How to get in trouble: If you really feel like playing with fire and risking upsetting Google (and Bing/Yahoo), the best way is to obtain incoming and outgoing links by buying and selling them.

Search engines — and once again, I'm referring to Google in particular — truly *despise* the selling of links. It sets off all sorts of alarms that something bogus is going on. Buying links, while not quite as dangerous as selling them, also tends to backfire.

Build your links naturally and organically. I'll quote directly from Google's language about link schemes:

The best way to get other sites to create high-quality, relevant links to yours is to create unique, relevant content that can naturally gain popularity in the Internet community. Creating good content pays off: Links are usually editorial votes given by choice, and the more useful content you have, the greater the chances someone else will find that content valuable to their readers and link to it.

As with SEO in general, there's more to generating great incoming links, but these are the basic tenets to keep in mind.

CHAPTER 2
Mobile Marketing

You'll recall that smartphones and tablets were *many, many* numerous times in the introduction.

Honestly, there's no way to talk about them *too much*. Because much like internet marketing is marketing in this digital age, the mobile internet isn't just the future — it's the present.

In 2021, we've reached the point where smartphones are utterly omnipresent in the United States and all developed countries.

Today, they're easy to use, affordable, and incredibly convenient. Ten years ago, they might have been mostly limited to people in their wage-earning years, but as I noted previously, teenagers (and even some adolescents) have their own smartphones. Grandparents and even great-grandparents have their own smartphones.

Of course they do. Grabbing your smartphone before you leave the house is as essential to your routine as putting on pants. (For some people, it's probably *more* important.)

If you have teenagers, you want to know you can contact them anytime they're out of the house — and that they can contact you as needed. If you have parents in their seventies or eighties, you want them to be able to call you as needed for assistance.

Over the past decade, and especially in the last five years, smartphones have become a staple of everyday life for every generation.

If you were born in 2000, you almost certainly have a smartphone. If you were born in 1980, you almost certainly have one. If you were born in 1960, you almost certainly have one.

Even if you were born in *1950*, there's about a 60/40 chance you own, and regularly use, a smartphone in 2021.

A 2021 survey by Pew Research Group found that 85 percent of Americans own a smartphone, up from 81 percent in 2019. (That's a very impressive statistical jump in just two years.)

Per the study, 95 percent of Americans ages 30-49 owned a smartphone, followed by 83 percent of those ages 50-64, and 61 percent of those over 65.

All of those data points have skyrocketed in just the past few years—for the 65-plus category alone, the 61 percent statistic represents a **15-point increase** since just 2018!

Long story short: The demographic you're targeting has already made massive strides in smartphone adoption, and that's increasing every single day.

All of which makes perfect sense. Think about when you got your first cellphone. Suddenly, your landline didn't make a whole lot of sense anymore. You now had a phone in your hand that you could take anywhere. What use was it to have a phone that was wired to a wall back at your home?

If you still have a landline in your home (you have one for your cemetery, of course), it likely serves as only as a complement to your mobile phone.

Similarly, the desktop computer is increasingly becoming only a complement to a laptop, smartphone, or tablet. Americans now access the internet *much more often on mobile technologies* as they do from home. And that's especially true of smartphones.

Kids today know how to operate an iPhone or Android phone before they even enter grade school. Adults in their thirties and even those pushing 40 have been accustomed to communicating through mobile technology for much of their adult lives.

And it's very important not to dismiss the effect of mobile technology on older generations. Even just 10 years ago, we might not have expected people over 60 to be interested in carrying mobile phones. In 2021, many have abandoned their landlines and use their mobile phones exclusively.

Mobile marketing takes many forms, but in essence, it's simply the process of marketing and promoting your business through mobile technologies (particularly smartphones), whether through your website, social media, text messaging, or other means.

This is where your audience exists now. While some still get their online information through desktop computers, mobile use has eclipsed desktop use for good.

Defining a broad term

The concept of mobile marketing preceded the explosion in smartphone and tablet use, but the term had a more limited definition, for the most part, previously.

For example, the first thing many people thought of regarding the term mobile marketing was text messages, more specifically **SMS**, which stands for short message service.

This later expanded to **MMS** (multimedia message service), which let companies text users who opted-in to the service with images, audio, and video. Both technologies remain aspects of many companies' mobile marketing campaigns.

Another aspect was the innovation of **QR codes**, which let a user to scan a 2D image with the phone's camera instead of typing in a URL or doing an online search.

By including these images on posters, signs, magazine advertisements, etc., the company provided a simple way for the user to go straight to a website to access information or buy something.

However, QR codes never caught on for broad use. (They do remain useful in certain niche roles, but only a few industries bother using them anymore, and I don't recommend their use for cemetery clients in 2021.)

The only codes consumers typically scan these days with smartphones are **UPCs** (universal product codes), which let them easily research products in retail stores. (They also come in handy for scanning food products in apps such as MyFitnessPal, letting users easily determine calorie counts and related metrics.)

Today, mobile marketing has taken on a much broader definition. It now encompasses the type of marketing and promotion you would do for PC users, but for people now accessing the internet on phones.

For example, many websites are built to display well on laptop or desktop computer monitors. You can view them in Google Chrome, Microsoft Edge, or Mozilla Firefox browsers to ensure they display correctly.

Those same sites, however, *display very differently when viewed on a smartphone*. They can be hard to read and hard to navigate on smaller displays.

This has led many businesses to create mobile versions of their sites. The site knows it's being accessed from a mobile phone and defaults to a mobile version.

Other businesses take this process a step further and create Android or iOS apps for their phones, letting the user simply tap an app to access functions of the business.

In 2021, it's *much more important that your cemetery website be optimized for mobile users* than for desktop users. That's not just an opinion: It's the way search engines such as Google do business.

A few years ago, Google officially implemented its **mobile-first index**. Here's the simple definition: When determining how highly to rank your cemetery website, Google places much more weight on the mobile **user**

experience (abbreviated as UX) than on the desktop experience.

In other words, if your site looks great and works well on a desktop computer but looks bad and is hard to navigate on a smartphone, Google *pushes you down in its rankings*.

If your site works wonderfully on a smartphone but not so well on the desktop, your site will rank better than the other way around.

Of course, I strongly recommend your cemetery website be optimized for *both* mobile and desktop users. That's especially important for cemeteries, because you'll still naturally have more desktop searchers (due to the average age of your target audience) than other industries will. For you, it's critical to have a great UX for both.

However, if you had no other choice but to choose one UX to optimize in 2021, *it must be mobile*. That ensures that best rankings in search results and the best overall experience for families.

Mobile marketing is *the* key tool for local businesses

Mobile marketing is most critical for businesses such as cemeteries, who do all (or *virtually* all of their business) *locally*. Because you have a physical business that relies on local customers, it's imperative that your marketing efforts not only *include* mobile, but literally make it a top priority.

As I indicated above, it's time to stop thinking of your website or your online ads as being seen most often on a large monitor attached to a desktop computer.

Please forgive the bold type that follows, but I don't want you to miss this point:

Those days are over. Just like Google, it's time for you to think <u>mobile-first</u>.

Because you have a brick-and-mortar business that relies on local customers, it's critical to be sure your marketing efforts not only include mobile, but make it a priority.

Some people will view your site on a desktop, sure, the same way some people were still listening to audio cassettes when the rest of the world was moving to compact discs, or how some still watched VHS tapes after DVDs arrived — and how a few stragglers are still listening to CDs and watching DVDs today, even though most of the world has moved past physical media and on to digital music and video.

Increasingly more people are viewing your site on a smartphone, and that will just keep growing throughout 2021 and beyond. Mobile SEO and Local SEO are now *virtually synonymous*.

If your cemetery's website isn't designed to automatically convert to a user-friendly mobile version when viewed on a phone, you'll lose virtually every customer who pulls it up on a smartphone.

Not only does it take a lot more effort to read a fully featured site on a small screen, but you'll be seen by the visitor as hopelessly behind the times. If your local competitors have mobile-optimized sites and you don't, you're at a massive disadvantage.

Mobile devices also make it extremely easy to monitor statistics on who's checking out your site and listings, when and where they're viewing it, and which visitors chose to contact you or otherwise convert into a customer. These analytics are critical to optimizing your marketing campaign.

The superhero of mobile marketing: hyper-geotargeting

At this point in the book, if you're still not quite convinced that I consider leverage smartphones to be essential to your marketing efforts, don't worry: I'll be repeating it several more times.

Actually, I'll go ahead and triple-down on it right now. I'll even break out the exclamation points and a different (and larger) font, because you need to hear this loud and clear:

> Americans of all demographics are carrying around <u>unbelievably powerful computers</u> in their pockets!
> They're <u>constantly</u> accessing the internet!
> They can go online <u>virtually anywhere</u> they travel — literally anywhere there's a mobile signal or a Wi-Fi network open to them!

Was that a little too much? Just be glad I didn't go with the bold type and comic sans font. (I considered it for a minute there.)

Here's why I was so forceful with those points: Cemeteries *in particular* can leverage the power of smartphones in a way many other industries can't, using one specific tool: **hyper-geotargeting**.

The term **geotargeting** has been around for a few years, and here's what it means:

Smartphones "broadcast" their locations in a few different ways. One of those is GPS, which is built in to the technology. But phones also use local cell towers and Wi-Fi networks to determine their exact position in the world.

It's true that a user can turn off location services in his or her phone, but the vast majority of people do not do so.

For one thing, a lot of people don't realize that's an option. For another, leaving on your location service provides the user many benefits — such as using Google Maps (or Apple Maps, on iPhones) for navigation.

If you remember dealing with those old folding print maps while trying to drive around an unfamiliar city, you appreciate how wonderful navigation services are. You just tell the maps app where to go, and it declares step-by-step directions. It's wonderful.

It can do this because it automatically knows *where you are right now* in addition to where you're going. It even provides the best route based on traffic data and current road construction projects!

So most people keep their location service on. And that's incredibly beneficial to marketers, because we can use that information to *specifically target people* when they're in *specific locations*.

Geotargeting itself isn't purely a mobile tool — it's really just a way of targeting people in a particular geographic area.

When marketers create Facebook ads or Google Display Network ads for a local business, for example, they typically limit the reach of those ads to a particular city or even ZIP code.

After all, there's no point to advertising your services in Los Angeles if your business only serves. Limiting the reach to a particular area also keeps your total cost much lower.

Hyper-geotargeting is the process of limiting your reach to an even smaller area. It could be a subdivision, a neighborhood, or even just a city block. It could even be an area not much larger than a single building.

By using this technique, you can limit your advertising to highly specific areas that fit the demographics of your audience: retirement communities, assisted living facilities, neighborhoods with large numbers of retired veterans, and so on.

But there's another aspect to hyper-geotargeting that works especially well for smartphones.

Because these devices constantly broadcast their location, you can use this tool to specifically target people who are attending a funeral service — some of the warmest leads for prearrangements.

Similarly, you could specifically target people who are at a hospital. Some of them might be in the market for your services soon, and many also will be receptive to your marketing.

Now, let me say that I realize not everyone will be comfortable with these methods. Some might find them a bit intrusive. I completely respect those concerns. If you don't think it's right for you, you don't have to include it in your marketing strategy.

With that said, I do encourage cemetery owners to consider using this tool. By leveraging the power of hyper-geotargeting, you're simply marketing your services to people who need them. And the ads you make available to them can (and *should*) be entirely respectful in tone.

You're just being surgically targeted in your marketing effort — which provides great ROI for you and communicates your excellent services to the proper audience.

CHAPTER 3
Social Media Marketing

Some people would argue the world was a better place when people could sit down in a restaurant and could resist the urge to look down at their phones every 30 seconds to see whether they had a new notification on Facebook (or Instagram, or LinkedIn, or Snapchat) or a new tweet on Twitter.

Regardless, that's a reality these days. Some people say they're addicted to their phones, and it's hard to disagree. They communicate constantly through social media, and that communication, as noted earlier, increasingly occurs through smartphones.

The giants in social media — Facebook, YouTube, Twitter, Instagram, and WhatsApp — wield astonishing power to let people and businesses interact with each other in real time. Having a presence on Facebook, Twitter, and Instagram, at the very least, is a requirement for any online business.

A cemetery, of course, is a little different. But it's not as different as you might *think* it is.

I'll elaborate on these points more in a bit, but here are a few things to know right from the top:

Yes, even a cemetery can properly make use of social media to market its services.

Yes, there are types of content you can publish that are entirely appropriate for the services you provide.

Yes, social media can be an enormous influence on generating more prearrangement contracts for your firm.

I'll come back to those points shortly. First, let's look at social media from a return on investment perspective.

The biggest benefit to platforms such as Facebook and Twitter is the cost: their basic functions are free.

Sure, there are paid advertising functions that can be used as desired, and you'll see a lot of benefit from "boosting" posts on Facebook, in particular, but it costs nothing to set up a basic Facebook page and start posting.

The same is true of Twitter. They provide a means to reach out to potential clientele at no included cost.

Of course, money isn't the only valuable resource to a business. Time is just as valuable, and the time expended on social media is a factor in its use.

Your cemetery business might be set up in a way where you can easily communicate regularly on Facebook or Twitter on a daily basis.

If it isn't, you might need to delegate those responsibilities to an employee or contract the process out to a third party, and those options require financial resources.

Whatever the case, every business should have a company page on Facebook at the very least. It's simply expected in today's digital world.

Having a Facebook page — and making sure to post on it regularly, even if it's only a short post or two every day — show that you're active and engaged in today's digital world.

Every time your company adds friends/followers on Facebook or Twitter, you're adding to your cemetery's branding and influence. Every time you blog about subjects relevant to deathcare and people comment on the posts or link to them, you're expanding your outreach.

However, there's one critical thing to understand whenever you use social media to market your business:

If you use it *unwisely*, such as being too focused on pitching your cemetery's services or spamming followers with commercial links, you're risking a massive backlash. There are few better ways to sink your social media marketing than by being too commercially oriented.

(If you recall the anecdote from the introduction about the cemetery that literally only posted to ask for donations, I'm sure you'll agree it's an even worse approach.)

People generally still don't use social media to be "sold to." They use it to interact and to learn about things of interest to them. There's a lot of room *within that construct* to promote your cemetery, but for the most part, it has to be done *without a hard sell*.

Use social media to make connections with interested parties. Share information, resources, advice, suggestions. You're a professional in the deathcare industry, so put that knowledge to use.

When people show interest in the services you provide, *that's* the time to provide information along those lines.

Social media can be an incredibly useful resource for business marketing when used wisely, but it can backfire quickly if you let the temptation of the hard sell get in the way.

Build relationships first; sell later.

Is a particular social network worth the time?

Not every social media platform is equal. Facebook and Twitter remain the superstars of the social media world, particularly for the demographics you're targeting in deathcare.

Instagram and Snapchat have grown massively in recent years, but their usage is strongest among younger generations.

In 2021, you're certainly not targeting Generation Z (those born in the mid-1990s to mid-2000s) for deathcare, so there's no reason to concern yourself with Snapchat (at least not yet).

Instagram skews a bit older than Snapchat, and it has stolen a big chunk of market share from Facebook among millennials (and to some degree, Generation X), but your core audience remains baby boomers and the silent generation. Thus I don't recommend prioritizing Instagram at this time, but it's certainly something to consider.

It's also fair to say that you can ignore TikTok, which is currently very popular among younger people but has no foothold in your target demographic at all (at least for now; we'll see what the future holds.)

Facebook is where you want to be. Although it has made some algorithmic changes that massively limit organic reach (which means how many people see your "free" posts), it remains the best platform for targeting your audience.

(With that said, the best social media strategy doesn't exclusively target Facebook users. It's never good to put all your eggs in one basket.)

There are only so many hours in the day, and as a small business owner, you need to be able to tell the wheat from the chaff. We've put together a few questions you should consider when determining whether a new social network will drive leads and make your phone ring.

Who is using the network now? Not who the platform wants to use the network. Not who it hopes will use the network. Who is on there *currently*?

You should be able to identify the demographics of the network, how and when its users are interacting with it, why they are using it, and how involved they are.

How likely are these people to use or promote your product? Even if the people using the network fall into your demographic, you need to determine whether they're likely to be interested in the services you provide.

Are these the type of people using the platform? Is the platform itself set up to easily share items of interest between people using it?

The networks that provide the best return on investment tend to be the ones in which social sharing elements are integral to the platform and consistently used.

Facebook

You know your creation has become a landmark aspect of popular culture when someone makes a major feature film about both your creation and you.

The Social Network might not have always portrayed Facebook inventor Mark Zuckerberg in the kindest light, but the 2010 film's very existence showed what a gigantic influence Facebook was in people's everyday lives.

That's true even as newer social media platforms such as Instagram (which is actually owned by Facebook) have stolen some of Facebook's mojo. Younger people, in particular, have fled Facebook in recent years, virtually considering it "their parents' social media."

Facebook's policies have also put off a lot of users over the past few years, somehow managing to upset people from both sides of the political aisle, which is no easy feat.

As quickly as things change, a future edition of this book in five or 10 years might be extolling the virtues of Instagram and barely mentioning Facebook. But that's the future, and in 2021, Facebook remains a major player.

Even as younger people have moved on from Facebook, the platform has *continued to grow in use overall*. That's right. In 2021, Facebook is far from dying.

Granted, the growth has slowed substantially over the past few years, and even as the platform picks up new users, it's also lost quite a few (for reasons that include those noted above). Regardless, the platform added 299 million active users in 2020 alone. It's up to about 2.8 billion users worldwide as I write this.

Facebook has become a constant companion in people's lives. And again, it's important to remember that Facebook is the more convenient, even the most *comfortable*, platform for middle-aged and older people.

Whatever its faults, it's also incredibly convenient and easy to use. Mothers and grandmothers love it for keeping up with their families and distant friends. They're not giving it up anytime soon.

Advertising on Facebook: The social engagement aspect of Facebook is obviously useful, but again, it has its limitations, such as the need to avoid a hard-sell approach.

Facebook paid advertising is an entirely different animal. The platform provides tools that let you place ads that will conform to people's interests across Facebook.

This isn't a good place to get into the specifics, for two reasons. First, it can be a bit complicated. Second, Facebook revises its advertising approach constantly, so best practices today could be very different by next week.

Whether Facebook advertising will provide a good return on your investment is something to consider thoughtfully, preferably with the assistance of an internet marketing professional. I can tell you that many clients have seen excellent ROI on thoughtfully crafted Facebook advertising campaigns.

Boosted posts on Facebook

For any type of business, having some sort of presence on Facebook is a must. It's a largely simple and completely free way to build your brand, market your services, and communicate to your customers.

Actually, let's get back to that "completely free" thing for the moment. Yes, it's still technically free, but as with any very successful social media platform, Facebook is looking to monetize its services.

If you use Facebook, you've probably noticed the ability to **"boost" your posts**, which costs money.

Boosting your posts lets you increase the time your post is seen by your friends, in addition to increasing the likelihood the post will be seen.

These days, Facebook really wants businesses to pay at least something for the promotion they get through the service. To that end, it changed its algorithm to massively depress the "organic reach" of posts on Facebook business pages.

In other words, the vast majority of unpaid posts you publish will not be seen in your followers' news feeds. It's unfortunate, but that's the deal. Recent studies show that organic reach today could be as low as *2 percent*.

For this reason, it's very smart to boost selected posts, particularly ones where you're communicating new initiatives or special pricing or services. Followers will see your cemetery as an expert in this area and likely turn to you for these services.

Facebook Search: What you need to know

Facebook's search function pulls up relevant information based on you (the searcher) — your interests, your pastimes, what you care about.

In other words, your search results will be different from those of other searchers, because Facebook already knows what you're interested in, based on your Facebook activity and connections.

Facebook hopes that instead of simply using Google Search to find businesses and people of interest to you, you'll use its internal search function, which it believes will get you what you're looking for faster and more efficiently.

What this means to your cemetery is that you should ensure you're active and well represented on Facebook, both on your own page and in interacting with users. That will increase the likelihood that people using Facebook Search will find your business.

Not only that, but you'll be prequalified by "Likes" from those users' friends and people within their fields of interest.

What's cool about Facebook Search is how it weights aspects that are similar to those of people (or businesses) to which you're connected on Facebook. For example, places that your connections "Like" or perform a check-in will show up higher on your search.

Facebook's search function makes the platform much more useful for marketing purposes, but as a Facebook user, you should also be aware that it makes information you might have considered private — or at least information you didn't necessarily want to broadcast to the world — far more easily accessible.

If you've "Liked" certain pages without much consideration, be advised that Facebook Search can show all that info *unless you've specifically restricted that information* in your privacy settings.

Similarly, if other people have restricted that information in their own settings, you won't get "hits" for them when you perform a search.

As I touched on above, there's been a lot of news the past couple of years about Facebook and privacy, in particular the ways it's been monetizing people's data, allowing questionable news to shape public opinion, and suspending users through a shadowy internal process.

If you're concerned about that, you're perfectly right to be. If you're especially worried about your personal data (on your personal Facebook page), you should use Facebook's privacy settings to limit the personal information you share.

You can even quit the platform altogether (again, as an individual) if you're truly apprehensive. I get it.

However, this book is about growing your cemetery business and how Facebook is powerful tool for doing that. So if you have concerns about Facebook in general, I suggest weighing those against the great benefits it can provide for your business.

To that end, you should use the Facebook Search function to make sure everything you want users to find when they search for local cemetery services will show up. That means getting your business's social profile in order.

Why? Because these social connections are pretty much the "links" that Facebook uses to determine relevancy and authority.

It's these photos, likes, check-ins, recommendations, etc. that the Facebook Search algorithm will use to qualify and personalize results for Facebook users.

In a very real sense, "Likes" are becoming the "links" of the new digital era on Facebook. What you Like defines you (and/or your business). The more you Like deathcare-relevant posts and pages, the better you'll do in Facebook Search.

Twitter

When Twitter arrived on the scene, business owners were skeptical about how useful this tool could be. If all you can do is post something in 140 characters, how useful can that be?

In fact, it turned out to be extremely useful, especially once it added options to let you write longer posts (with the remainder represented by a link), to include link shorteners (so your characters weren't all used up by a huge link) promoted accounts and posts, etc.

Back in 2018, Twitter finally expanded the character count on basic tweets themselves, letting users post up to 280 characters. For reference, the very paragraph you're reading right now (including spaces) is 247 characters. That's plenty of room!

At its heart, Twitter provides a great opportunity to communicate with customers in real time. Because most people use Twitter on their phones, you can connect with followers when they're out and about. And I probably don't need to remind you (again) that virtually everyone is on a smartphone these days.

Because the people who see your tweets are those who already follow you (or have retweeted your tweets to *their* followers), you have a largely *prequalified audience* for your tweets.

And, of course, just like Facebook, it's totally free to tweet anytime you like. (Twitter's promoted posts, just like Facebook's boosted posts, cost money.)

Advertising options for Twitter include **promoted tweets**, which let you promote your cemetery by targeting users who are similar to your current followers and those who have searched terms related to your types of services.

Promoted accounts appear in the "who to follow" section and in search results, appearing on the pages of users that would likely be interested in your brand.

There are other options as well, but what's right for you will depend on what you're looking to achieve.

Even if you don't use Twitter's paid options, it's an amazing way not only to communicate with families in your area, but also to receive immediate feedback. People who won't take the time to send an email are happy to fire off a quick tweet to let you know their feelings about your services.

Also, satisfied families can provide great word of mouth in seconds by tweeting to their friends whenever they have a great experience.

If someone does have a bad experience and posts about it on Twitter, at least you'll know about it right away and have an opportunity to make it right.

Yelp

Yelp was one of the first platforms to mix user reviews with a social media aspect, and it remains one of the biggest.

Although its usage has dipped a bit in recent years, as of this writing Yelp still averages more than 178 million unique visitors every month.

Throughout Yelp's existence, it's at times been an enormous benefit to local businesses — and also a huge pain in the butt. Most businesses have experienced both sides of the coin.

The concept is simple: After people go to local businesses — a doughnut shop, a motorcycle repair shop, a fine restaurant — they post a review on Yelp. These reviews help other people decide whether to frequent the establishment.

If every single Yelp user took care to provide a fair, unbiased, thoughtful review of the particular business, everything would be hunky-dory. You could read through the reviews and determine which ones you felt were most accurate and legitimate.

However, like everything else on the internet, people will try to game the system. Some people try to get perks from the establishments in exchange for a positive review. Some business owners try to run down their competitors with unfairly critical reviews, simply making up facts as they go.

And some people, even if they're not trying to game the system per se, just don't take the time to be very thoughtful when reviewing an establishment. If they just happened to be having a bad day, they might rip apart a place (figuratively) even if everything actually was satisfactory.

Yelp has taken steps to deal with all of these issues, and how effective those steps have been might depend on your perspective. The company has created systems to help weed out bogus reviews and keep them from being posted.

If Yelp isn't sure that a review is legitimate, the review gets trapped in the "Yelp filter." A user can only see these "not recommended" reviews by clicking on a specific link. (A big frustration for businesses, of course, is that sometimes legitimate five-star reviews gets trapped in the filter, like a dolphin in a tuna net.)

As for bogus reviews, they're not necessarily always negative: Business owners have been known to sign up under several different accounts and review their own establishments — providing glowing reviews across the board, of course.

The ascendancy of smartphones — you knew they were going to come up again — has only made Yelp more powerful.

Its local search capabilities make it easy to find places near where you are at a given moment and see reviews for those places. You can see why the veracity of those reviews is so incredibly important to business owners.

With all the concern about the veracity of Yelp pages, is it worth it to even participate in the process?

The answer is yes.

Online reviews are not going away, and neither is Yelp. You can't keep people from reviewing your cemetery, like it or not, so you might as well play along. By getting involved, you can help ensure you're being seen in the best light.

As you know, most people aren't going to contract with a cemetery on a whim. They want to have plenty of information first.

It goes without saying that having several excellent reviews on one of the internet's top review sites provides you a big advantage over local competitors who have negative reviews or simply too few reviews. That's why you can't afford to ignore your reputation on Yelp (or other major review sites).

I should note one more very important fact:

Yelp no longer lets businesses directly solicit reviews from clients and customers, unlike some other review platforms (including Google), so you must be careful not to overtly ask families to review you on Yelp.

I'll talk about Yelp more in this book's chapter on reviews and reputation, so for more information, head over there.

<u>Blogging</u>

While this is another area that might sound uncommon for a cemetery, the benefits of having a business blog are almost too great to mention.

Blogging about these issues in a way that displays expertise provides you enormous credibility, which goes a long way. It lets you communicate about what's going on with your cemetery. It provides people the opportunity to provide feedback and ask questions through comments.

(And you can moderate those comments before they're posted, removing the risk of spam or other problems.)

Then there's the SEO consideration: When you're generating a lot of content for your website that's relevant to deathcare, your SEO increases *massively*.

Having a strong, regularly updated blog is one of the very best things you can do to increase your website's traffic and search engine rankings.

Blogging also helps you create incoming and outgoing links, which are great for SEO. You can (and should) link to other relevant sites and articles in your blog posts. When you post something of interest to others, it's likely your post will be linked to (or shared through other platforms), increasing your incoming links and traffic to your site.

With all that said, there are some obvious potential downsides to blogging. Spelling, grammar, or fact errors in your posts can make you look unprofessional, so if you're not a good writer (or sufficiently detail-oriented), you should have a better-suited employee or a contracted professional do your blogging for you.

Alternately, you might be a great writer, but you just don't have time to blog. That's another reason to consider delegating the posting process. Whatever the case, the benefit to blogging is almost always worth finding a way to make it work.

Another concern relates to content. Many websites have gotten in trouble (appropriately) with Google for simply duplicating content from other sites in their blog posts.

Not only is this unethical (and in certain circumstances, illegal), but it's a great way to prompt Google, Yahoo, or Bing to drop your search engine ranking into the sewer.

Let's take a second to underline that point: ***Don't copy content from other sites.*** You also shouldn't buy content that clearly wasn't originally written for your site.

Even if you change around a few words here or there or "spin" the copy (a computerized process that rewords sentences), Google has ways of finding it out.

Write original content whenever possible. Posts don't necessarily have to be long; even a couple of paragraphs can be enough, as long as the content is focused on something that interests your target demographic: middle-class to upper-class Americans of middle age or older.

At RRM, we create original content for deathcare clients that covers a lot of different topics of interest to the AARP crowd. It's really not too difficult.

If you *do* want to share information from another site, no problem: Simply write a sentence or two in a post and link to the site where the article or post appears. You can even excerpt a small amount of the other post, but the key word in that sentence is *small*; too much will get you in trouble.

And whenever you use someone else's content in an excerpt, be certain to include attribution and a link.

As with everything else, blogging is more beneficial for certain types of businesses and services than others, but it has some benefits no matter what you do. Just its ability to improve your site's SEO alone is a good reason to try it.

If this sounds like too great a time investment, speak with a marketing consultant about possible options to outsource the process.

A lot of people make their livings blogging for a variety of different sites, and depending on your needs, these services can be very affordable, especially given the return on investment.

LinkedIn

A social network specifically for business professionals: a simple enough concept, and one that's worked out for LinkedIn to the tune of more than *740 million* members. (That's 240 million more than it had when I wrote my previous deathcare book in 2018.)

Don't get too hung up the term "business professionals." You don't need to wear a suit and tie to work to benefit from LinkedIn. That's how pervasive it has become for business networking.

LinkedIn simply makes it incredibly easy to allow registered users to maintain a list of contact details for people with whom they have some level of relationship. These people are called **connections**.

Once you've made connections, you can connect with people connected to them, allowing you to easily expand your networking base with people in your industry or with common interests/work histories.

You can create a comprehensive profile with a full resume and qualifications, and when you're looking for a new employee or business partner, you can search through LinkedIn users for the experience, skills, and qualifications you're looking for.

LinkedIn also lets you endorse people you've worked with (and be endorsed by the same) with the tap of a key. Having your business and various skills endorsed by well-connected users is obviously a great way to gain new business and new opportunities.

Here's the usual caveat: LinkedIn is most beneficial for businesses in which professional networking is an integral part of doing business. However, the platform has a lot of additional tools that can be useful for virtually every type of business owner.

LinkedIn doesn't require constant participation, although the more you participate on the platform, the more helpful it can be.

At the very least, having a LinkedIn profile for yourself is a great way to put your best foot forward and display your skills and abilities to people who might not otherwise know about them.

For a cemetery, linking to other providers in the industry and those who provide related services (albeit not your competitors) can provide a great foundation for organically building incoming links.

When their sites link to yours, it improves your traffic and your organic SEO, because Google values incoming links from companies in your field very highly.

Google My Business

Your Google My Business page is your virtual business identity in the Google universe. To be able to interact in the Google Plus social network and have followers share your business, you need to have your Google My Business identity set up and ready to share.

GMB has certain social media aspects, including the ability to include your own Google Posts in the platform

— something I strongly encourage you to do. It's excellent for engaging with your audience and helps your overall branding and website SEO as well.

I cover GMB rather extensively elsewhere in the book, so I won't go on too long here about its social media aspects. Suffice it to say that YouTube is the only Google-owned property that's been successful as a social media platform.

The social media success cycle

Ultimately, I hope you choose to include social media in your marketing plan, as it's rapidly becoming expected for all small businesses, including cemeteries.

If you do so, understand that investing in social media isn't as simple as publishing a couple of posts (or tweets) every day. In fact, there are four key aspects to what's known as **the social media success cycle**.

To get the most from social media, you have to eventually participate in all four aspects. Posting is only an element of one of these.

The four quadrants of the social media success cycle are:

Social listening: monitoring and responding to customer service and reputation management issues

Social influencing: establishing authority, most often through the distribution and sharing of useful content

Social networking: associating with authoritative individuals and brands, effectively creating a "rising tide that lifts all boats"

Social selling: generating leads and (ultimately) sales from prospects

I'm sure you've noticed that "selling" is the last one on the list, and that might seem strange. You might be wondering why you would invest time and related resources in social media if the goal isn't to drive business through sales.

The short version is that *social media isn't really an immediate sales generator*, at least not for most businesses.

When you dive into social media, don't presume you'll suddenly see a rapid influx of calls. This is a big-picture strategy. It's business development for the long haul.

And that's also why social selling comes *last* in the process. As I said, people don't want to be hit with a hard sell on social media.

The successful strategy is to gain their interest, *then* gain their trust, then weave in occasional pitches for your services. The "sales" posts must be a small percentage of your overall messaging. Otherwise, you lose trust your followers' trust — and then *you lose the followers*.

Let's go over each one of the four aspects:

Social listening: This is where you're listening and responding to your followers' comments on your social media platforms.

Cemeteries obviously don't get nearly as many of these as other types of businesses do, but that doesn't mean you can afford to ignore the ones that *do* appear.

You might get positive comments from families you served or questions about your pricing or services. You might get inquiries about special services for veterans. You might be asked how you accommodate mourners with physical disabilities.

What's important is that you're regularly checking your social media accounts for these comments and responding to them *quickly*. You never want a comment to go 24 hours without some sort of response, even if it's only a thank you! If you can reply even sooner — within 12 or even 8 hours — that's even better.

Much like responding to reviews (which I'll get into later), responding to social media comments makes it clear that you're focused on customer service.

Remember that you're not just responding to the original commenter. Your response will be viewed by all of your followers. This is an opportunity to brand yourself as a burial and cremation provider who's responsive and engaged.

Social influencing: This is the "posting" part of the process. It's where you're sharing content that's useful to the AARP audience and others who are interested in the services you provide.

You might be wondering why people would follow a cemetery on social media if they're not actively considering interment services. And that's a fair question. It wouldn't be honest to say you'll pick up followers as easily as businesses in other industries.

However, if you are providing useful content—and again, that can include health and fitness tips, financial planning for seniors, vacation ideas, etc. — you *will* see your following grow over time.

And as that following grows, you *will* be able to weave in the "social selling" aspect, marketing services to your followers.

Social networking: This is an often-overlooked part of the process. It simply means that you want to create connections with other businesses and associations related to deathcare and similar topics.

Of course, I'm not suggesting you network with direct competitors in your area. However, you can follow the major deathcare associations, and hopefully they'll follow back. You can comment on *their* social media platforms, helping promote your brand and increasing the likelihood you'll get a follow from them.

You also can create connections with businesses in your area you partner with or are affiliated with your line of work. This could include local veterans' associations such as the VFW or American Legion. It might also include local hospitals or hospice organizations, if they're okay with that (your mileage may vary in this area).

As usual, I suggest you think a little outside the box here. Try to network with social accounts that aren't so obviously connected to deathcare. Consider local health and fitness groups, for example.

Remember that you want to be viewed as providing an important service to your community (as you certainly are).

And of course, if you partner with certain noncompeting businesses, be sure to network with them as well.

Share these partners' posts when appropriate. The increases the likelihood that they'll share your posts. It's a lot like having internal and external links on your website. The more connections you have, the more you're seen as your community's local expert. It's a fabulous way to build your brand.

Social selling: Yes, this is the ultimate goal. You'll see benefits (especially in branding) from the other aspects, but at the end of the day, you really want to be selling your services through your social media.

And that's fine. Just keep in mind that if you sell to your followers *too soon* or *too often*, your follower list will dry up faster than a puddle in Arizona in August.

Patience is a virtue here. Try not to do *any* selling for the first few months of your social media plan. You're creating a foundation of trust you can build on later.

When you do include sales-oriented posts, keep them nuanced and light, at least at first. Just pepper them in now and then. No one will be put off by the occasional sales pitch; everyone knows you're a business, after all. You just never want it to be more than 10 percent (or preferably, only 5 percent) of your total posts.

Remember, you want your social media to enhance your online reputation. You want it to show you as an authority on helping families in your community. You want to show an interest in helping people live better lives, particularly in their elder years. You want to be seen as a business that reaches out thoughtfully and professionally when anyone notes a concern or has a question on a social media platform.

That's your ultimate goal. When you do all these things, you're viewed as the important community resource you are, not simply a business.

That all sounds like a lot, I know, especially for a small cemetery with only a handful of employees. I'm not here to tell you that a full-fledged social media plan is an easy thing to implement on your own, because it's not.

Realistically, you'll either need to hire someone who's pretty good at social media to implement this for you or contract out to a reputable marketing company. That's the most efficient and cost-effective way to ensure it's done right.

I'd just caution you to carefully scrutinize any agencies that make big promises of rapid profits from social media. It doesn't work that way (in deathcare, at least). Much like SEO, this is something you need to build up over time, but it will provide substantial results if you stick with it.

Section 2:

Conversions

CHAPTER 4
Maximizing Website Conversions

Perhaps you're thinking: *Of course* my cemetery has a website. I pay a few dollars every year or two to the domain provider and hosting company.

My phone number is on there, along with photos of the land and buildings, some images of monuments and memorials, maybe even a couple of paragraphs about what we do. I've done my due diligence.

Well, that's just the bare minimum. That's like putting on shoes because the grocery store won't serve you otherwise.

Simply having a website is like simply having a business. It exists. Now what are you going to *do* with it?

Like every other aspect of your business, your website has a purpose. We can refer to that purpose in general ways. But it all ultimately comes down to one thing: *conversions*.

I touched on conversions earlier, but let's dig in a little deeper:

People define "conversions" many different ways. For businesses where the goal is online sales, a conversion is a very simple thing: a sale. It's *converted* a visitor into a paying customer.

As the owner of a cemetery, you earn revenue through providing services such as burials and cremation. These things take place in person. So it's not as easy to gauge how effective your website has been in converting visitors by using basic sales analytics.

However, there are many analytical methods to determine how effective your website is at attracting new visitors and determining how they got there, how long they spend on the site, what pages they click on, and how long they spend on those pages.

These tools let you see which images, videos, and links they click on. And they let you know what's working (and what's not working) in appealing to new clientele.

I've said it before, and I'll say it again: People are now finding services (and products) online far more than ever before. If they want to find a dog walker, a bike shop, or a psychic, they're finding them *online*.

Businesses that have no website at all? They're in massive trouble — even in a traditional industry such as deathcare. To the ever-growing digital population, those businesses don't exist.

Businesses that have a bare-bones website? They're almost as invisible as those with *no* website. With little-to-no content, no SEO to attract visitors, no incoming links to provide inroads for potential customers, a website like that is a needle in the proverbial haystack.

Businesses with a middle-of-the-road website? That's 100 times better, no question about it. If it has some content, some degree of SEO, and uses some links — and if that's tied in with a touch of social media — that website is actually achieving the minimum standard of what's needed to be successful in 2021 and beyond.

However, you can do better. The jump from a bare-bones website to a middle-of-the-road one is huge, no doubt. It's like going from a Burger King to an Outback Steakhouse.

It's the next step that makes all the difference, the one that jumps from a chain steakhouse — a perfectly serviceable chain steakhouse, but a chain steakhouse all the same — to a five-star restaurant.

That's the step to a website that's actually oriented toward *converting visitors into clientele*. And yes, it can still be designed in a way that's tasteful and respectful, which is so important in deathcare.

This is one of the most powerful revenue generators in modern business. And obtaining this goal is a lot easier than opening a five-star restaurant. (There's certainly no need to hire a fancy executive chef.) By employing a set of very basic tools, you can turn your cemetery website into a powerful revenue generator.

If you're going to have a website, you might as well put it to work for you. That's what it's there for. If you're not maximizing its potential, you're leaving an incredible amount of money on the table.

Designing your website for conversions

Here's the first thing to understand: No visitor will convert to a client until your site has *proven itself*. Every element of the site must underline your professionalism and credibility.

It must say to the visitor: *We're the right choice for you. There's no need to shop around; we are the solution to your problem.*

That's why someone's visiting your site, right? Someone needs to solve a problem.

If you can convince the visitor that you're the best choice right then and there, you've removed any need for the visitor to leave and keep checking around. *The visitor wants you to be the solution.* You just have to make it happen.

Only after you have proven yourself to your visitors can you focus on converting visitors to paying customers.

Use great testimonials: You have many satisfied customers, right? (We're talking about the *living* ones, to be clear.) Ask a few to write a testimonial.

Visitors want to know that real people have been incredibly impressed by the professionalism and care you showed when they've dealt with your business. Trust is obviously a powerful consideration in deathcare.

You can include more testimonials elsewhere — devote an entire page to them if you like — but use the best ones on all pages where you're trying to compel the visitor to contact you regarding services.

Of course, testimonials are effectively the same as online reviews. I'll get into reviews and reputation later, but you should know that the more great reviews you receive, the better you'll convert website visitors.

Address your visitors personally: The personal touch is very important, especially in your industry. People want to know you're a real person who's proud of your business.

Put together some copy (or hire someone with copywriting experience, if need be) to tell your visitors who you are, how important your profession is to you, and why you're the best person to help them.

Never forget that *your goal is not to sell someone on something*. It's to *help* the person in need, to resolve whatever related issue that person has at this time. (They might sound similar, but there's a key difference: Put yourself in the visitor's shoes.)

Show why the visitor should work with you: Here's where you explain why your business is the best option.

Think about why someone should choose your cemetery over anyone else. It's like writing a resume or a cover letter when you want a job: The employer has a problem (a job opening) that needs filled, so you're explaining why you're the best person to solve that problem.

Just as in a resume, don't get too bogged down in details: Focus on the most important facts that sell your cemetery on the visitor. Whenever possible, include as many *quantifiable* facts as you can.

This can be a hard nut to crack, but it's absolutely worth the time. Brainstorm with your staff and really figure out why you're the best option for helping your community in times of need. What sets your cemetery apart? What is your **unique selling proposition** (USP)?

Once you know this, you can drive that point home on your cemetery website. Know your USP and really impress upon the visitor. That's one of the best ways to drive conversions.

And here's another one:

Call to action: There are some other copy elements that can help reinforce your pitch, but they can vary depending on a number of factors, so let's cut to this integral aspect:

Your site needs a very clear **call to action** (CTA).

Most often for a cemetery, that call to action will be soliciting the visitor to call your telephone number. If the visitor does so through a click on your website, it will be convenient *and* trackable.

The CTA could be to click on your email address link (it *must* be clickable — *always* make it easy for the visitor), which is another thing you can track.

The CTA also could be to fill out an information form — again, that's for people interested in preplanning. (Keep this form short and sweet; that's what you'd want when you visit a site.)

Impress upon the visitor that you're the best option for them, and the solution is just a phone call (or email) away.

Improving your calls to action

The CTA is one of the most important aspects of your website or landing page. You attracted a visitor to your site for one reason: to act in some way.

Everything on your site must be oriented toward converting that visitor. Here are a few ways to improve your calls to action:

Include the CTA on every page on your site: You never want people to have to search for your phone number or email address. Make it easy. If your website it designed so that the CTA is a stable element throughout the site, the visitor can interact with it at any point, on any page.

Specifically, this means you want your web designer to create a **fixed header** (aka a **sticky header**) that stays put throughout the navigation experience. If the user scrolls down on a particular page, this header remains in place. If the user navigates to another page, the header remains.

In addition to ensuring the CTA is clearly displayed throughout your cemetery site, this creates a uniform look and feel. No matter where the visitor travels, your business name and contact information are boldly displayed at the top.

Make sure your CTA stands out: You obviously don't want anything on a cemetery site to be obnoxious, but make sure your CTA stands apart. Whatever your CTA is, make sure it really "pops" out. And yes, it can be polite and respectful but still be distinctive from everything around it.

For text CTAs, use a different color for hyperlinks so it's clear to readers that the text is clickable and an action can be taken. For visual CTAs, use a color that starkly contrasts with the rest of your page.

Use strong, active language: This isn't the place to be passive or longwinded. Everything is funneling toward the visitor taking action, so make the CTA clear, simple, and direct.

The visitor should understand exactly what he or she is getting and why acting on the CTA (whether filling out a contact form or calling/emailing you) is the logical thing to do. If that isn't being clearly conveyed, make a change.

Be sure the value of acting is obvious: If you can't explain to a visitor why your offer is going to help in some way, why would the person click through? Your visitor came to the site to gather information about deathcare services: The CTA needs to be the solution.

The need for (page) speed

Like Maverick and Goose in the iconic film *Top Gun* (if you want to feel old, that movie came out *25 years* ago), it's time to feel the need:

The need for speed.

You don't need to be a U.S. Naval Aviator (or enjoy Kenny Loggins songs) to appreciate the importance of speed. You just need to have a website that you hope will rank well in search results, generate traffic and convert well.

I'm including **page speed** in the website conversions chapter because that's where it plays its most critical role, but it's also a key part of your SEO.

If pages on your cemetery website don't load fast enough, Google (and other search engines) will punish it in search results.

In 2018, Google made page speed a huge priority. Since then, it expects the content on business websites to load quickly, which is essentially what we mean by page speed.

To be more specific, page speed equates to "page load time," which means how long it takes to fully display the content on a specific page.

So why is that so incredibly important right now for your cemetery website?

Let's set aside for a moment how important it is to Google and just focus on **user experience** (UX).

Here's the nutshell version:

Slow website speed kills conversions.

According to a survey by Kissmetrics, about half of visitors now expect website content to load in *two seconds or less*. More than *40 percent* of visitors will abandon a website if the content takes more than *three seconds* to load.

That's where consumer expectations are in 2021. Three seconds might not sound slow at first, but try counting out those seconds (one one-thousand, two one-thousand, three one-thousand) when you first visit a website. You'll appreciate how slow that feels in modern terms.

Unfortunately, many older websites for cemeteries, particularly independent ones, don't meet that mark.

And that's just the *minimum* expectation. Again, most American consumers expect content to load within *two seconds*.

Per the survey, every extra second it takes for content to load reduces conversions about 7 percent. So if your content takes three seconds longer to load than it should, you're *losing more than 20 percent* of potential conversions on your cemetery site.

So you already have user experience problems if your content loads too slowly. That's just half of the equation. The other concern—and it's a big one—is that slow-loading content also hurts you with Google.

Google has been factoring page speed into its organic search rankings for a while, but it really ramped up that factor in 2018, in particular because so many people now visit websites on *mobile devices*.

This goes hand in hand with Google's mobile-first index, which makes the mobile performance of your website Google's baseline for determining rankings.

In other words, there's no time to lose: Your cemetery website needs to be fast, and you must work quickly to make it so.

Speed is the word of the day in every sense.

So why is this happening? Well, Google is constantly tweaking its ranking algorithms, so it's not exactly a surprise. But whenever it does so, its objective is to reward (with better rankings) websites that are providing the *best experience* to users.

The faster content loads, the better the experience. Now that people in every demographic are now researching business services (including deathcare) more on mobile devices than on desktop computers, Google knows the mobile experience is the top priority going forward.

PageSpeed vs. page speed: These terms look identical, but there's a slight difference between them.

I already covered "page speed," the general term. The other refers to **PageSpeed Insights**. That's a free Google tool to measure the performance of a page for mobile and desktop devices. It uses that performance to assign your site a score.

PageSpeed Insights doesn't provide an *exact* indicator of page speed on your site, but it's quite beneficial. By following the suggestions provided by the tool, your content will load faster, and thus your site is more likely to be ranked higher in local search and other rankings.

Go to PageSpeed Insights to see how your cemetery website fares. It's as simple as typing in your site URL (or pasting in that URL from the address bar when you view your home page).

The tool will provide a numerical score on a 100-point scale. It also will display a variety of optimization suggestions for how your content can load faster.

If your score isn't impressive, don't waste time: Discuss the issue with your website provider ASAP. If the provider doesn't act immediately to get your page speed up to snuff, that's a big problem.

This issue can't wait. Your cemetery website could be facing a serious drop in local rankings if its speed doesn't make the grade, and you'll be missing out on website conversions from the traffic you *do* get.

Secure your site

Consider this situation: You're an everyday American searching online for a cemetery. You find one and click the link.

In the address window, you see this ominous message from Google:

Not secure

Not secure? What does that mean?

It might not concern some people, but others, in their confusion and/or fear, will immediately "bounce" out of that site before exploring further.

That's really bad news if it happens to your cemetery site. You're certainly not going to convert visitors if they bounce away as soon as they arrive!

Unfortunately, that's the situation a lot of independent cemeteries face. Even in 2021, many are still using old-school **HTTP** technology instead of the far more secure **HTTPS**.

I'm sure that sounds confusing, but don't worry, I'll break it down in a moment. Before that, to help you understand how critical this is, let's look at how many of your website visitors could be affected by this.

A couple of years ago, Google wanted to push websites to upgrade to HTTPS, which (in a nutshell) provides users much more security over information they provide. So it now displays a "Not Secure" warning in the URL field of its browser, Google Chrome.

While that particular change only affects sites viewed in Chrome, you'll note that it has *65 percent* of the browser market share — so close to *two out of every three searchers* will be viewing your site in Chrome.

Also, rival browsers such as Internet Explorer and Microsoft Edge (both from Microsoft) and Firefox (from Mozilla) are rapidly following suit.

Even if the "not secure" warning only scares off one out of four visitors (a very conservative estimate), that means you just lost *of your unique visitors* in a flash.

In this digital age, with more people searching for burial and cremation services every day, that kind of drop-off can sink a cemetery.

HTTPS explained: Essentially, HTTPS indicates that all communications between your browser and a particular website are *encrypted*, and thus much safer from hackers and other malicious actors. In addition to encryption, HTTPS providers protections for authentication and data integrity.

Technically, HTTPS stands for "Hyper Text Transfer Protocol Secure," which just means it's the *secure* version of the HTTP protocol. HTTPS pages are typically encrypted either with the SSL (Secure Sockets Layer) or TLS (Transport Layer Security) protocol.

Yes, I know that all sounds incredibly complex, and no, you don't need to remember all those details. Just know that your website must be HTTPS, not HTTP.

How do you know whether your cemetery website is already using HTTPS?

It couldn't be easier.

Simply open your website in Chrome and look in the address bar. If it's HTTPS, you'll see "https://" at the start of the address. You'll also see a padlock icon with the word "Secure" on the left edge.

If it's *not* HTTPS, you'll likely see nothing except the main domain name (e.g., "thisisafakedomainname.com"), possibly preceded by "www."

Sites that are not secure also display a small information button (a lowercase "i" in a circle) on the left side. Clicking on that, visitors get a message that reads:

"Your connection to this site is not secure. You should not enter any information on this site (for example, passwords or credit cards), because it could be stolen by hackers."

Does that sound like something *you* want to convey to potential customers? I didn't think so.

If you've had your website for a long time and haven't done any redevelopment for a while, you're likely in this camp. Just searching local cemeteries across America for five minutes, I found more than a dozen that do not run HTTPS, so it's a big concern.

If you're not already using HTTPS, here's what to do: While it's true that converting from HTTP to HTTPS is inexpensive and really not very complicated, it is complex enough that it's best handled by a seasoned IT professional.

A major mistake in the transition process could impede your website's functionality or even render it useless. Even if it there's no harm to the functionality, a subpar transfer could hurt your site's search engine optimization (SEO) and/or user experience. So it needs to be done right.

Google wants to protect online users, and it considers HTTPS a foundational aspect of doing that. In fact, it typically *ranks HTTPS sites better* than HTTP sites in organic search — another great reason to make the change.

If you want to generate more website conversions, you need to make sure people who arrive at your site actually "open the door" and come inside. You can't convert anyone who turns tail at the doorstep!

A brief overview of contact fields for lead/client generation

Your landing page for preplanning has one absolute goal: Generate clients, or at least get leads that you can convert into clients. The most integral part of making this happen is including a form in which your visitor can provide contact information.

That sounds like a simple enough affair, but how effective your lead generation is actually can depend heavily on how this form is designed.

According to recent surveys, most marketers consider the lead-capture form to have a very significant impact on website performance.

You have a very short window of time to capture anyone's attention when that person visits your page — many experts put this window at a mere *six seconds*.

This rule is something to consider when designing your lead generation form. If the form seems too arduous or time-consuming to fill out, most visitors won't even bother.

(Most people aren't exactly thrilled about considering their own mortality in the first place, so why make it even more burdensome?)

The key is finding a balance between getting the information you need and keeping the form simple enough that it won't scare off your visitor.

Some studies indicate that indicated that the optimal number of fields to include is seven, but I don't agree.

Keep it simpler than that. Get a name, phone number, and email address. Just three fields.

If you really want to ask for a physical address, I understand, but including that field possibly could scare off the lead.

I prefer the strategy of getting basic info at first, "warming up" the lead through marketing emails and related techniques, and then working to obtain a physical address.

If you include too many fields, you'll see a significant drop-off in conversions. If you include too few, you're in danger of missing out on valuable information you might need.

Whatever you do, don't get into the double digits: That's as good as telling visitors you don't consider their time valuable. They're providing you information, not taking the SAT.

Keep in mind that there's a big difference between what information you'd *like* to have and what you *need* to have.

Name, email address, and phone number are essentials, obviously. For your type of business, you *might* ask for a ZIP code and/or and some other demographic information, such as household income or age range.

But again, the more fields you include, the fewer conversions you're likely to get.

Ultimately, one of the best things you can do is review your landing page as if you were simply a visitor: Would you want to fill out that form? What advantage will you get from providing your contact info?

If your responses aren't overwhelmingly positive, you'll want to make some changes.

Grabbing your website visitor's attention right from the top

Visitors are great, right? Well, maybe not visitors to your home, at least when they're annoying in-laws or someone selling appliances door to door. But getting visitors to your business website is great.

If they're coming to your site, you're popular. You can check the analytics and see where they're coming from and what brought them there.

Of course... visiting the site is only half of the process, and you don't get any credit for half. A half-baked cake isn't something you want to eat. A half-vacuumed carpet just looks worse than a carpet that hasn't been vacuumed at all. You know what they say: Close only counts in horseshoes.

As I noted previously (yes, I repeat myself when something is *really* important), visitors do you no good if you can't convert them into clientele.

It's like having the most-visited art gallery in town, but if no one ever buys a painting, you'll be the most popular artist begging for quarters on the street.

Your site can't just be focused on attracting visitors — it needs to *actively sell* those visitors on what you can exclusively provide them. It needs to get the point across right away.

How do you do that on your site? For one thing, figure out your top selling point to customers and try to make that the first thing they see.

Your business's name is all well and good, but that alone doesn't sell the customer (unless your business is named Bill Gates' Free Money for Everybody Inc.).

Use that valuable real estate at the top of your site to sell your visitors on what your cemetery does better than anyone else: your *USP*.

Again, I realize that a cemetery website should always be respectful and not have a "hard sell" feel, but there are definite ways to impress your qualities upon the visitor without seeming crass.

Whatever you do best, whatever your claim to fame, spell it out clearly and make sure visitors can't miss it. If that's the best price, the best services, whatever it is, *don't be shy about it.*

A note about SEO: As I noted earlier in this book, an integral aspect of ranking highly in search engine results is incorporating relevant keywords in your copy.

These need to be in there, but far too many sites use keywords incorrectly. They stuff copy full of keywords to the point where the writing sounds like it's intended for the spiders (the search engine software that crawls the site), not for the visitor.

Never do this.

It will send visitors racing for the "exit." It looks especially amateurish on a cemetery website, but it honestly looks bad no matter what business you're in.

A qualified internet marketing expert can help you learn how to incorporate keywords so they sound natural in the copy.

Also, when keywords are used *too* often, this can actually *hurt* your SEO. Counterintuitive as it might seem, clunkily jamming in "cremation" or "burial services" into every single paragraph works *against* you.

The search engines will penalize your site in the rankings if the keywords appear too often, or not in the right places.

Yes, it's important to serve two masters, the human visitor and the search engine spiders, but always err on the side of writing intelligent, compelling copy for the visitor.

Nothing will undermine your credibility faster than copy that makes little-to-no sense because it's only there to drive search engine rankings.

Conversion optimization factors

Let's go over some additional factors that help ensure conversions on your website:

Structure your navigation: On too many websites, the site navigation is cluttered and disorganized; it doesn't help drive potential customers to the pages that will give them the information they need. One of the biggest mistakes is creating site navigation that links to virtually every page on the site.

When you provide so many options, it's confusing to the visitor, and you're not taking advantage of the opportunity to lead the visitor through a page-by-page process to deliver the message you want to convey. It's like suggesting a reader jump around randomly from chapter to chapter in a novel.

No matter your site's size, try to pare your navigation down to as few elements as possible. It's okay to have a dozen links or so in your navigation, but be sure they are *organized* in a way that helps visitors easily choose the right page.

Implementing structured navigation makes it much easier for visitors to quickly find the pages that are most interesting to them.

A cemetery website doesn't have to be overly complicated. You want to make sure there's good, detailed content on every one of the pages, but that doesn't mean you need a lot of pages.

The easier you make it on the visitor, the more likely you are to get a conversion. Carefully scrutinize every part of your site and see where you can simplify the process. Of course, a good marketing firm can be a huge help in this process.

Make sure your site has a voice: If your copy sounds like every other cemetery site, you're missing an opportunity to differentiate your business from the competition.

While the tone of your website's copy should always be professional, "professional" doesn't have to mean "antiseptic."

Too many people believe that business-oriented copy needs to read like the most academic of research papers. *This is a huge mistake.*

Copy can be professional but still sound *resonant* and *personal*—even on a cemetery website.

Read through your copy and see if it sounds like you're simply having a casual conversation with a potential client. That's the tone you want. The more personal flair you can inject in your website copy, the more it will stand out from the vanilla sound of so many other cemetery sites.

Having a unique voice gives you an edge. It tells potential clientele that you're different, and when they are choosing between you and a competitor, that might be the advantage that makes them choose you.

Provide a box that lets visitors search your site: This depends on how well your site has been developed, but if you have good, useful copy on all your pages, a "search this site" feature can be a great boon.

If you're not sure how well your site delivers results when people search for certain common terms or phrases, test its functionality yourself before letting the feature go live. A search function that works poorly is worse than no search function at all.

If you do have a great site search that gives perfect results every time, this can help visitors find specific products, features, or information quickly without having to scan a bunch of pages.

This search data can also be helpful in telling you what people are looking for, allowing you to better promote those areas. Better promotion of your services means *more conversions*.

Be consistent in formatting (fonts, bold, italics, images): There should be a consistent look and feel to all your pages, making them seem (as they are) all part of the same message.

While some homepages may look a bit different than the internal pages, it is important to be consistent from one page to the next. Your primary navigation should not change from one page to the next, nor should your footer, page layout, colors, etc.

When you don't have that kind of consistency, the onsite experience can be quite jarring, and this can ruin the experience for visitors. Any bad experience is bad for conversions.

Make sure your site is optimized for mobile: I covered this extensively earlier, but I'm just noting it again here because it's absolutely *essential* for conversions.

While cemetery sites still get more desktop traffic than most other industries do, you'll still be getting at least half of your traffic from mobile devices. Depending on where you're located and how tech-savvy people in your area are, you might already be getting more mobile traffic than desktop traffic.

No one using a smartphone wants to deal with an old-school website that isn't optimized for mobile. They want to call you with a single click. They want to be able to view what you offer and look over your services in a clear, easily viewed format.

If you're not optimized for mobile, you could be throwing away *half or even more* of your conversions. Remember, conversions create clients, and (of course) clients create revenue. Can you afford to just wave goodbye to all that business?

Delivering great conversion copy

I hit upon a number of content considerations earlier in this section, but let's talk a bit more about persuasive copy and how it can convert visitors into customers.

More isn't always better: Don't overload your pages with thousands of words of copy. You're trying to deliver a message, so provide just enough information to get that message across, and then get out of the way. You don't want to bury the visitor with minutiae that don't build your brand or deliver a conversion.

However... don't take that to mean that a couple of paragraphs on each page will get the job done. Your copy needs to be detailed enough that people clearly understand what you're conveying and accept you as your area's top expert on deathcare.

If you have a Frequently Asked Questions (FAQ) page, be through, but resist the urge to pack it with tons of salesy language. Provide honest-to-goodness answers to actual likely questions.

For the most part, keep sentences short and to the point. Don't repeat information that you've covered elsewhere on the site. (I realize that's ironic, considering how often I've doubled down and even *tripled* down on important points in this book. But there's a good reason for that.)

Your visitor's time is valuable, and digging through long stretches of copy to find necessary information will cause a visitor to look elsewhere. Everything is a balancing act: Provide strong, detailed, concise information, and then wrap it up.

Did I make it perfectly clear that you shouldn't skimp on content? Content really is king, and the higher quantity of strong content you have on your site and your pages, the higher the traffic and conversions, generally.

Content-rich sites also attract more links, which is always a good thing (presuming the links are legitimate and relevant). Be sure to have plenty of content; just make sure that the content you have is broken up into *clear, concise, easily digestible* chunks.

Show that you're trustworthy: Why don't people convert even though a site clearly shows that it can provide a definite solution to the visitor's need?

Usually, the biggest roadblock is that the site hasn't *sufficiently communicated its trustworthiness* to the visitor. I'm sure it's rare that you get a client who picked a name out of a hat for something as important as deathcare services.

Because far too many bad businesspeople have promised too much and delivered too little in the digital age, online customers tend to have their shields up. They're afraid of wasting money, wasting time, putting their money on the wrong horse.

Your copy should be consistently focused on putting a potential customer's mind at ease. Certain guarantees can help with this. Testimonials (both written and especially in video, as noted earlier) can help with this.

The visitor wants to believe you. The visitor wants to benefit from what you have to offer. As the business owner, you have to conquer that concern in the visitor's mind that you might not be legitimate.

Trustworthiness, transparency, credible authority, lots of high-value content, and plain old decency: These are your best weapons.

These factors would be true of any business, but they're obviously critical for a cemetery.

People might buy some gizmo online if it's really cheap, even if they're not 100 percent sure the seller is entirely trustworthy. They might grab a burrito from a random food truck at the park if they're famished, holding out hope that it won't make them sick.

But they certainly won't work with a cemetery they don't trust completely. It's your job to make that perfectly clear through the information you include on your website.

Everything on your site needs to show you can be trusted. Provide real contact information. Display your photograph. Include pictures of your business. Include a short video featuring you and your staff. Make visitors feel like they've already visited your location before they've even set foot in it.

If you're a Better Business Bureau member, make note of that (and display the seal). If you're affiliated with national deathcare industry organizations, put their seals up there. Display positive reviews and testimonials. That's what we call **social proof**. It's a key aspect of ensuring more website conversions.

Trust, trust, trust. That's what you're selling.

Check the readability of your copy on various browsers, including mobile browsers: Nothing will run off a visitor faster than a website that's hard to read. The fonts and colors you use might look wonderful in Google Chrome but awful in Mozilla Firefox or Microsoft Edge.

Test the readability of your site in all types of browsers and select options that display clearly (and in a compelling way) across the board.

And of course, make sure the site is optimized for mobile — and that means it displays and functions well on both iPhones and Android devices.

While SEO is important, always put the human visitor first: Yes, I'll repeat myself one more time: If your copy reads like it's intended for search engine spiders and not the reader, *you're not going to convert*. This practice massively undermines your credibility and serves to confuse the reader. Get your keywords in there, but be certain that the copy in personable and conversational in tone.

Finding the balance in copy that's compelling for readers yet also keyword-rich is an art of its own, and a good internet marketing expert and copywriter can be a great help with this.

Onsite organic SEO

Effective SEO isn't simply a matter of getting your site to rank as highly as possible in SERPs or driving as much traffic as possible to your site.

You want people coming to your site who want to purchase your particular services. If the visitors who arrive aren't interested in deathcare services at this time, they're obviously not going to convert into clientele.

Effective SEO delivers the *right* people to your site, people who are likely to convert. To achieve this, you want to use relevant keyword phrases not only in the copy people read, but also in the coding of the site itself.

This requires making use of **meta tags**, which help inform the search engines of what your site is all about. Of course, appropriate use of meta tags also gives your

SEO a big overall boost. Search engines are better able to index these pages, providing a big increase in visibility and rankings.

Meta tags are HTML tags you place on the coding of the page. They can include **title tags**, **description meta tags**, **heading tags** and **image tags**, among others.

Certain types of site software provide toolkits that make it easier to add these tags to your site without messing around with HTML — the most basic website programming language.

Title tags: These are extremely important indicators that inform search engines what your page is about. Things to keep in mind:

The title tag is not to be confused with your *page heading*. It's part of your meta data and the title users see at the very top of your web browser. It's also the title people will see for your site on a SERP.

Google typically only displays the first 50-60 characters in a title tag, so don't go over 60 (including spaces). Because you have a limited number of characters, your title is precious real estate. Think like a user and type in search terms you know the user will use.

Some users will only look at titles, so your title needs to be something that will compel the user to click through when your result shows up in SERPs.

Titles for each page also must be unique; they cannot be repeated anywhere else on your site. The best SEO practice is to include your keyword in your page title, preferably at the beginning of the title.

For your industry, as with all tags on your site, something specific to burial and cremation obviously should be incorporated.

Meta description tags: These describe what your page is about and are displayed along with your title in search results. Obviously, how your site is described will be a huge influence on whether a searcher clicks through to your site.

Google will display 120-158 characters (including spaces) for a meta description, so again, don't make it too long. Make it something that's direct and compelling, and include words that users are likely to use to find the page.

Get your primary keywords in there, but avoid keyword-stuffing, and also try to include a call to action such as *read more about...*, *find out...*, or *learn all about...*.

An enticing description will increase your click-through rate. It also lets you stand out from other sites that show up in SERPs.

Heading (H1) tags: These tags are intended to indicate the most prominent (and presumably most important) text on a page. These are followed by other H tags, H2 through H6, ordered from most important to least. These are important from an SEO perspective, but they also make the page easy to read.

Think about a magazine. Important things, such as the magazine's title or a front-page feature, would be in

H1. A smaller article's title might be in H2 and a subtitle in H3.

Google expects a webpage to be laid out with a series of headers that makes sense to the reader. These tell Google and other search engines what is most important.

It's important not to go overboard on H1 tags, just like you don't want to go overboard on things such as bold or italics.

Emphasis is used to *differentiate* things as being more important than other things; *if everything is "important," then nothing is*.

Abusing H1 tags will definitely get a webpage penalized by Google and other search engines, so creating multiple H1 tags on a page purely for the purpose of trying to improve your search engine ranking is definitely frowned upon. It's generally best to stick with just one H1 tag per page.

Image tags: While both human visitors and search engine spiders can interpret words on a page, images themselves are (for the most part) only able to be interpreted by actual humans.

To let the spiders know what's being seen in an image, you need to add image tags. These are also known as **alt-image tags**, because the text you include in them will be shown to your human visitors if the image fails to load for some reason.

Search engines crawl these tags as well, so by including your deathcare-related keywords (when natural and appropriate) in these tags, you're once again improving your SEO for people who search for these keywords.

As usual, don't stuff keywords into tags willy-nilly, because that can blow up in your face.

An additional way to improve image SEO is by giving the image's actual file a descriptive name. Instead of something like "IMG0042.jpg" for a particular type of casket, rename the file something like "Star-legacy-cherry-casket.jpg." The hyphens allow search engines to recognize the composite parts as individual words.

Section 3:

Reviews and Reputation

CHAPTER 5
Customer Review Sites and Reputation Management

The internet lets you tell everyone in the world how awesome your services and/or products are. You can go on about your incredible customer service on your website. You can develop advertisements that boast about your being the very best cemetery in your neighborhood or city.

And if that spiel is legitimate, worded well, and backed up by testimonials from happy customers, people will most likely accept that your assessment of your stellar reputation is genuine.

However, there's another side to dealing with reputation issues in the age of the internet:

You're not the only one who gets to weigh in on your business.

Whether you like it or not, members of the general public will have their say on their experiences with your company.

As I noted earlier, customer/client review sites exist to aggregate information from people who have tried out a business and wish to write a review.

While some people enjoy writing reviews of almost every establishment or service provider they interact with, most only take the time to write a review if they had a spectacular experience — or a truly horrible one.

For this reason, businesses need to be ready to do a great job for every customer.

That's not a bad idea in theory: With its online reputation potentially at stake every day, a business presumably will make a point of doing a great job with every customer interaction. That's extra impetus to go the extra mile, and it's better for the customers as well.

Of course, like anything else on the internet, reviews can be gamed.

As terrible as it sounds, certain less scrupulous business owners try to artificially inflate their positive reviews by registering on these sites under a variety of different names.

Even worse, these business owners often *pan* their local competitors — whether or not the criticisms are deserved — under other names. (Thankfully, this doesn't happen as often among cemeteries as in other industries, but it certainly happens occasionally.)

Also, unfair reviews are sometimes posted by people who don't necessarily have a stake in the businesses. Some people just get a kick out of ripping companies —

again, regardless of whether such criticism is actually warranted.

Others try to trade super-positive reviews for free stuff, discounts, upgrades, and other perks. All of these underhanded strategies can influence the legitimacy of online reviews.

Because of this, most of the major review sites, along with Google, set up algorithms that are intended to seek out and hide or remove reviews that are false or illegitimate. These algorithms have had mixed results, but they've at least applied some controls to a process that can be fraught with misbehavior.

The major sites also include some options to allow businesses to contest unfair or inappropriate reviews, and all let the business comment on reviews that appear, providing the company an opportunity to place the criticism in context and (if desired) to communicate a desire to address any legitimate concerns that were noted.

I'll talk about some of those options in a bit, but what's most important to take from this is that *you must be vigilant in reviewing your business's online reputation.*

This means paying attention to whatever people are saying about your business on review sites, in blogs, in news reports, and anywhere else.

People who contract for something such as deathcare services are more likely to post about the experience — whether positive or negative — than someone who simply bought a bagel from the coffee shop down the street. (Granted, there are people who do this, and we wish them all the best.)

If a reviewer hits you with a particularly negative review, it's *critical* that you not let it sit out there without any comment or response. If several bad reviews go unanswered, that can be *extraordinarily damaging* to your reputation. No one wants to contract with a cemetery that's been shredded in online reviews.

Remember at the start of this book when I explained how more and more people every day are getting information about local businesses from their smartphones?

These devices make it unbelievably easy to quickly check out reviews when a potential customer pulls up your Google listing or a Yelp app. And remember, Bing also integrates Yelp reviews into its searches.

These days, when someone simply clicks on your business in a maps application or does a search for nearby businesses and comes across yours, those reviews are sitting right there to be read.

No matter how well you promote your cemetery, if several negative reviews pop up any time someone check you out, your business is in big trouble.

You absolutely *can't afford to ignore online customer reviews*. Good ones can be incredibly helpful, but bad ones can be devastating.

You *must* proactively generate positive online reviews. They're critical for business success.

I realize the process requires more nuance in deathcare, but it can be done. Many cemeteries have been very successful at it—it's simply a matter of dedicating yourself to the process and initiating it.

But before we go any further, we need to talk about:

Review Gating

Yes, it's a strange term. Don't worry, I'm about to explain it.

Review gating refers to the process of using specialized software to filter out potential negative reviews and only let people publish positive reviews of your business.

The typical process works like this: You send an email to a customer (in your case, either a loved one's family or a prearrangement client) asking whether they were satisfied with the services you provided and whether they'd like to publish a review.

If they were completely satisfied, they're guided to a clickable link where they can easily write a quick review.

If they were *not* entirely satisfied, they're guided to clickable link that lets them contact you directly about their concerns — bypassing the publishing process.

Obviously, this let businesses avoid negative reviews by "heading them off at the pass." Which is why Google banned the practice in 2018.

You don't want to be involved in this process, because as I noted before, the last thing you want to do is upset Google. If you get caught, you'll be penalized.

With that said, there *are* software options that allow people to publish negative reviews is they wish, but they *also* provide the option to reach out to the business first.

By doing this, a dissatisfied client has the opportunity to address concerns before reviewing, if so desired, but is not actually barred from leaving a negative review.

We've found that many families are fine with contacting a cemetery directly before leaving a negative review, and after working things out, they either choose not to leave a negative review — or actually leave a positive one! At RRM, we have proprietary software that facilitates this process.

If a marketing agency claims it can make negative reviews "disappear" or entirely block them from occurring, don't work with that business. No one can legitimately promise that.

However, there are means by which you can negotiate with people who have left negative reviews and often get them to remove the review or even choose to modify it to be more positive.

Also, all review platforms have processes for removing truly fake reviews. (I go into fake reviews a little more later in this chapter.)

While there are lots of review sites online — some of which exist only to cover particular types of businesses or niches — here are the main players:

Yelp

Google reviews have cut into Yelp's dominance a bit, but the latter remains the big daddy (or big mommy, take your pick) of review sites.

As one of the first sites to marry local search, user reviews, and social networking aspects, it's grown astronomically since its founding in 2004, and its reach has expanded with ridiculous speed in recent years.

Yelp also has a reputation system that lets visitors see which contributing users are the most popular, respected, and prolific. This can help visitors judge how legitimate reviews from these users tend to be, among other things.

Business owners can also communicate with contributors who post reviews on their page through messages or public comments.

Having reviews of your cemetery on Yelp — especially positive reviews — is a boon. That's been true since the site launched, but it's especially true now.

As I mentioned earlier, the idea of a review aggregation site compiling plaudits and criticisms of various businesses is a controversial one.

Some business owners have questioned Yelp's own credibility, especially after allegations emerged that some Yelp salespeople might have offered to hide negative reviews of businesses that paid for advertising sponsorship contracts. Yelp has refuted these allegations, but they're pervasive enough to be concerning.

Certain businesses also question the effectiveness of Yelp's review filter, which is intended to prevent and remove illegitimate reviews. In certain cases, the businesses claim, reviews that would seem to be clearly false show up next to "real" reviews. In others, honest-to-goodness legit reviews get snagged by the filter and are not displayed.

In the same way that Google won't disclose the specifics of its search ranking algorithms to prevent them from being gamed, Yelp won't disclose the specifics of its review filter algorithms.

Several class-action lawsuits have been filed against Yelp by businesses that have had positive reviews removed but have been unable to get negative reviews similarly redressed.

The fundamental allegation in most of these suits is that Yelp is trying to force businesses to advertise (which is how Yelp makes its money). However, as of this writing, there have been no court decisions proving or even suggesting that Yelp has acted inappropriately.

One frustrating factor with Yelp is that it no longer allows businesses to directly solicit reviews. It wants satisfied clients to decide entirely on their own to review a business.

I don't recommend trying to work around this regulation, because if Yelp catches you soliciting reviews, it can penalize your cemetery on its platform.

With that said, there's nothing wrong with asking satisfied families for reviews in general, and if *they* ask whether to do so Yelp, there's nothing prohibiting you from saying "that's fine."

Advertising with Yelp: While the company continues to contend that advertising with Yelp won't affect the display of organically created user reviews (either positive or negative), it seems safe to assume that advertising on Yelp can't hurt.

At the very least, the company makes no bones about the fact that your Yelp page will be better promoted and get more visibility if you're an advertiser.

However, that increased visibility might not be worth the return on investment for most small businesses. Many marketing experts believe Yelp's paid ads currently cost far more than what you receive in return.

The numbers can get a little confusing if you're not familiar with **cost per impressions**, which is the model Yelp uses for the ads. Much like traditional advertising, an *impression* merely means that someone has *seen* your ad. You're paying for the ad regardless of whether someone clicks through to your site.

Cost per click, by comparison, only costs you money if someone clicks through.

With Yelp ads, the cost per impression (CPM) is exponentially more expensive than it is with standard CPM advertising. It's also much harder to track how effective your advertising is when you can't get click-through numbers.

Yelp is also requiring a one-year commitment for its most favorable rates, which aren't particularly low in the first place.

In general, I don't recommend Yelp advertising at this time for most small businesses, including cemeteries. If you have plenty of extra marketing money to burn and want to give it a shot, it's an option to consider. But I think you'll get better ROI from other initiatives.

Google reviews/Google My Business

I covered GMB extensively earlier, so I won't get into it deeply here.

The thing to know is that people can review your business through Google, and these reviews are incredibly important. With the vast majority of people using Google to research local businesses, these reviews are among the most prominently displayed to users.

The quality *and* quantity of Google reviews your business receives also plays an indirect role in SEO. The short version is that Google's spiders can tell which businesses are reviewed a lot, so they grant those websites more authority. And more authority means higher search rankings.

Note that if you haven't verified your business with GMB yet, your information won't necessarily show up on Maps, Search, and other Google services. Additionally, *only verified businesses can respond to reviews*.

So if you're not sure whether you've gone through verification, stop everything (seriously, just put this book down or close your e-reader) and do it right now.

Google systems are integrated by default into all Android-based devices, so you want to have the best reviews possible on your Google listing.

When someone Googles your business, your verified GMB listing typically will appear on the right side of the SERP. One of the first things people will see is your Google review rating: your overall score (on a five-star scale) and how many reviews you've received.

While it's great to have a handful of five-star reviews, surveys have shown that it's actually better to have a *higher quantity* of reviews, even if they're not all five stars!

In other words, people generally have greater trust in a business that has (for example) 25 reviews with a 4.7 overall rating than one that has seven reviews with a perfect five-star rating.

You always want five-star reviews, of course, but don't let "perfect be the enemy of the good," as they say. Work hard to generate *a lot* of Google reviews.

Like Yelp, Google My Business uses a reviewer algorithm to ensure the display of the most legitimate reviews.

Google provides an option to flag reviews as inappropriate if they violate its guidelines, but as with Yelp, it can be hard to simply have a negative review removed if it falls within the guidelines. You can respond to a negative review with comments to provide your side of the issue.

Garnering more reviews

While negative reviews obviously are bad for your business, the best way to counter them typically is to solicit reviews from satisfied customers. They're obviously far more likely to rate your business positively, and as I noted before, the quantity of reviews your business receives will provide a huge boost to your rankings in local search results.

Like it or not, there's no way to get rid of online reviews. They're simply a reality of the times. So instead of fighting them, do your best to get the most great reviews you can. Ways to do this include:

Solicit reviews on your website: I mentioned before that Yelp prohibits businesses from directly soliciting reviews, so don't do that. However, there's nothing wrong with asking satisfied families to review you on other platforms.

You can create a page on your site specifically intended for reviews, and that can have a simple form they can fill out. The easier you make it for the customer, the more likely you are to get a review — particularly a positive one.

I should mention, once again, that a site that provides deathcare services should consider the importance of subtlety and respectfulness in this process.

Add a review request to invoices and receipts: While putting the request on a printed form isn't as user-friendly as other methods, because the customer will have to then go online to do the review, it's a good complementary option. Also, if you use digital invoices or receipts, those can include a link your customer can use to easily go straight to filling out a review.

Put it in an email: Again, including a simple link to your own review form or that on a popular platform (such as your page, Yelp, etc.) makes it easy for the customer. Just be sure you're being careful not to spam your customers with emails, which could very easily prompt *negative* reviews.

Monitoring and responding to positive and negative reviews

It's never fun having your services criticized, regardless of whether the feedback is fair. When it comes to an online review, the impact of a complaining customer is far heavier than that of a card in a customer feedback box. It can imperil your business now and in the future.

This is why it's so critical to stay on top of how your business is being reviewed online. Remember that *reviews are good* for your business in many ways, so you shouldn't just put your head in the sand or take actions to stay under the radar. You do a good job, and your customers know this. The key is to get them to make this known, as I discussed in the previous section.

One thing you absolutely must do is *monitor all reviews you receive.* It's not as hard as it sounds. In fact, there are services available that can help monitor all the major review sites and let you review them together, and your internet marketing professional can help with this. If you don't know what's being said about you online, you're powerless to adapt to it.

While it's most important to respond (and respond *quickly*) to negative reviews, the importance of responding to positive reviews is often overlooked.

When people take the time to say something nice about your company, they like to know that you've seen the review and appreciate it. Thanking them and promising to do a great job will go a long way toward attracting new clientele.

Also, if the only reviews you respond to are the negative ones, that leaves a poor impression on everyone who sees that page.

Thanking people for glowing reviews and responding positively to critical reviews will always paint you in the very best light.

Granted, it can be challenging at first to find a positive tone in replying to a negative review, but it's not too hard once you get used to it.

After a cooling-off period, respond privately to the reviewer: You don't always have to start off with a public comment. On Yelp, for example, you can reach out to the critical customer first through a private message. Perhaps the criticism resulted purely from a misunderstanding or miscommunication that can be worked out.

Whatever the case, give yourself a little time to let your emotions ebb. It's natural to be upset by a negative review, but resist the temptation to overreact.

Instead, take a deep breath and evaluate the customer's complaint. Determine what has been (or can still be) done to address the issue. Engage the customer with a short and positive private response — either through the online review platform or via email — that recognizes the customer's criticism and discusses ways to remedy the situation.

By taking the issue offline, you can prevent a potentially ugly back-and-forth discussion that could draw even more unwanted attention to the review.

If you're successful in resolving the issue offline, you can politely ask the customer to revise the review to note that the complaint was addressed or even delete it altogether.

If that doesn't help, provide a public reply: Even if you work things out privately, the reviewer might not elect to revise or remove the original negative review. Don't badger the reviewer; this might only lead the reviewer to further criticize your company on a follow-up comment or another review.

If you believe the issue was resolved, note that you reached out and successfully addressed the customer's concern. You might also include what steps you took to ensure satisfaction — for example, that a discount was offered or a replacement product provided.

If you believe there were legitimate inaccuracies with claims made in the review, offer a short response that corrects the facts. Again, keep it positive and professional. Maintaining the high road and appearing conciliatory to customer concerns is more important than establishing "your side."

Another thing to consider is that you should do everything in your power to discourage negative reviews in the first place (while encouraging positive ones).

The foundation of this is simple: Do great work, provide great customer service, and generally make everyone who works with you feel happy and satisfied.

However, no matter how well your cemetery is run, there will always be customers who are unhappy with the product or service provided. That's just the nature of business and the broad spectrum by which people interpret their customer experience.

Some people are easy to please; others never seem to be satisfied. Two people could have the exact same experience and interpret it two completely different ways.

Customers who are unsatisfied often turn to online review sites to voice their frustration. Some wish to warn potential customers about your practices, some want to damage your company's reputation out of spite, and some hope to receive a response that could include an invitation to revisit the work or provide a discount or refund.

Many times, the customer will note concerns directly with a business before choosing to post them publicly. It's critical to seize this opportunity while you still have a chance to allay these concerns. Respond quickly and work out a resolution before a negative review is posted.

In most instances, staying positive, reassuring the customer that concerns will be addressed, and reaching some sort of compromise — even if that requires a rebate, refund, or other concession — is far preferable to the negative word of mouth a negative online review can generate.

Over time, these reviews can cost you much more than what would be involved in proactively remedying a customer's complaint.

Dealing with fake reviews

Just because a review is negative, that doesn't necessarily make it *fake*.

As I noted earlier, both positive and negative reviews can be entirely legitimate, and both positive and negative reviews can be entirely fake.

Some unscrupulous business owners create fake positive reviews of their own business. Some also create fake negative reviews of their competitors. They often get caught doing one and/or the other, but not always: As we all know, life isn't fair.

I'm sure I don't need to tell anyone reading this book that you should never create fake reviews — either positive ones for your own firm or negative ones for others — but that doesn't mean you can count on everyone to do the right thing.

In the big picture, the best way to counteract the effect of fake negative reviews of your business is to generate lots of positive reviews for own cemetery.

But that doesn't mean you can't act on these bogus criticisms. They unfairly drive down your overall ratings, hurt your reputation, and just plain stick in your craw.

It's one thing if you miss an important detail and are legitimately dinged for it. We're all human; things happen. But you shouldn't just sit quietly and tolerate unfair reviews of your business. Your reputation is too important.

Before you act on a fake review, do your due diligence: Make sure it's fake. Some people are more sensitive or nitpicky than others. If a legitimate client was upset over a minor issue and criticized your firm for it in a review, reach out empathetically and try to resolve the issue. Hopefully you'll get an updated (and far more positive) review out of the process.

But don't try to have it removed if wasn't actually fake. Pressing Google, Facebook, or Yelp to remove a whole slew of reviews for no legitimate reason will just make you "the boy who cried wolf." Then you won't have a leg to stand on when you need a truly fake review to be pulled.

When you're *sure* a review is fake, here's what to do. For these examples, I'm using Google, but similar approaches work for other review platforms as well:

1. Ask Google to remove the reviews

When reviews violate Google guidelines or are obviously spam meant to attack your online reputation, Google might remove them upon request.

If you receive a sudden onslaught of reviews with obviously fake names (or no names at all), or they include content that violates Google's terms, report them. You might also have luck making a case that you couldn't have served the reviewer — for example, noting that you have no record whatsoever of serving a family in the situation the reviewer complained about.

2. Respond to the reviews

Google doesn't always remove fake reviews. If someone enters a name for the review, gives you one star, and doesn't leave any review text, the reviewer is *technically* not violating any Google terms. You might still be able to have it reviewed by the platform (it's worth a shot), but there's no guarantee.

Consider combating these reviews with professional, concise responses that explain you don't have a record of service that matches the review. Then ask for more information so you can address any issues.

3. Publicize the negative review to your audience

Normally, you want to limit exposure to things that might damage your brand online, but if reviews are obviously fake, the families you've graciously served — and members of your community who know you're a reputable firm — are likely to side with you.

Share that you received a fake review on your social media pages so families considering your services know the review claims aren't true. A common positive side effect of this tactic is that families who were satisfied with your services in the past may be prompted to leave a positive review. That actually happens quite often.

The worst thing you can do when faced with negative Google reviews (fake or otherwise) is to ignore them. Cemetery owners who quickly act on their Google reviews are seen as professionals who care about their brand and local families.

CHAPTER 6
Email Marketing

Think about the most tech-wary person you know, a true technophobe through and through.

Can you think of anyone? Someone who has truly let the digital revolution pass him by. Doesn't have a smartphone, much less the two (or even three) some people carry today. Doesn't have a laptop, much less a tablet. Has no interest in Twitter, doesn't care about Facebook, wouldn't know Yelp from yogurt.

At the very least, your friend almost certainly has a home PC and uses email.

In reality, almost everyone in America uses email and checks it regularly. Even people who rarely leave home check their email on a constant basis.

Most modern email systems provide pop-ups and alerts to let you know you have a new email. Preschoolers have it. Great-grandmothers have it. With postal rates continuing to rise all the time, people continue to shift from communicating by snail mail to email.

And even if you don't own or use a smartphone, it's a fair bet your mobile phone — even one manufactured a decade or more ago — has the capability to receive and send email. Your email provider is most likely free to use, making it all the more valuable. Email access is easy, it's free, it's omnipresent.

Of course, email also produces a lot of spam, which is another thing entirely, but I'll get back to that.

Email marketing can be tricky in some ways, but it's a marketing initiative no business can afford to ignore. You have a free way to communicate with your prospective customers who opt-in to your emails.

Can emails sometimes get lost in the morass of communications people get in their inboxes every day? Sure, but no less than direct mail advertising gets lost in the stack of junk that piles up in the mailbox. And direct mail costs *money*.

Email is by far the most cost-effective way to deliver marketing messages for your cemetery business. You can send personalized, targeted, and interest-specific messages to a large number of people.

But there are other advantages. You can include links in email that prompt the recipient to click through directly to your site/landing page. Also, studies show that more than 80 percent of the email you send is opened in the first 48 hours after delivery, so you can get a fairly immediate response or action based on it.

First, avoid spam

Before getting into some email strategies, let me repeat something I touched on earlier:

Never spam.

Never, *ever* spam.

If you're sending out a mass email you think *might* be spam, it's almost certainly spam. Don't send it.

Sending out unsolicited emails is the very best way to get your business identified as a spammer, ensuring your emails a permanent grave in the ever-more-sensitive spam filters developed by Gmail, Yahoo mail, Hotmail/Outlook, etc.

When was the last time you even *checked* your spam filter, much less actually clicked on something you didn't recognize in it?

Spam emails are typically automatically deleted every 30 days or so for good reason: They're not beneficial, and no one wants them.

Even if your unsolicited email sneaks around the filter and reaches a recipient's inbox, most email providers provide a one-click method to report an email as spam.

If your email looks spammy, you can expect this to happen.

Oh, and one other thing: *spamming is technically illegal*. So there's that.

Sticking with professional email standards keeps your emails legally compliant and ensures great relationships with the people who receive your emails.

An internet marketing professional can help you understand all the ways your email could be classified as spam, though they mostly fall under common sense. Even if you always send emails to people who have opted in, there are two critical things to consider:

To send commercial emails that don't violate the law, every email should include two things: the *physical address* associated with your business (a P.O. box is accepted as long as it's associated with your business's actual location), and an *unsubscribe option*.

The unsubscribe process also has to be accomplishable by replying to a single email or by visiting a single web page.

You're also required by law to remove anyone who unsubscribes from your email list permanently within 10 days of the unsubscribe request. You can't add that person back without the recipient's explicit permission.

Getting permission

If you haven't received permission from a recipient, your email almost certainly will be considered spam. So always get permission.

Technically, there are two types of permission: **implicit** or **explicit**.

Implicit permission occurs when someone shares his or her email address with you for some reason, such as filling out a contact form on your website for more information regarding a particular service or item.

That's opened the door for you to contact the person for that reason, but you haven't actually asked permission to continue to contact the person down the line with product offers and the like (unless that's clearly noted when the person signs on).

It's much safer to get explicit permission: Tell the person what to expect when by providing an email. If you plan to send promotions and other communications, be straight about it.

Once you've compiled your list (more on that in a moment), don't share it, don't sell it, don't trade it. Those are surefire ways to destroy your reputation with your customers.

Do I really have to be that careful? In a word, yes. As few as two spam complaints per 1,000 customers can prompt internet service providers to block you from sending emails to their customers.

Even when you've received explicit permission, your emails can be interpreted as spam depending on how they're constructed or how often you send them.

In a sense, it doesn't matter whether the recipient asked you to email in the first place. If the emails appear too frequently, don't appear legitimate, or don't provide useful information, they can be interpreted to be spam.

Putting your list together

It's harder these days to compile a large list than it used to be, which is understandable: People are more careful about giving out their email address for fear of getting crushed by communications every day. Ever overlook an important email because it was buried in a bunch of inbox chaff? It's not a fun feeling.

In reality, you don't need a huge list for your email marketing to be effective.

The best lists contain the names of loyal repeat customers, referral sources who respect others' privacy, and interested prospects who know you and your business well enough to recognize (and want) your communications. Ultimately, *quality* is much more important than *quantity*.

Unless your list is going to be extremely short, it's best to use some sort of database (or software specifically designed to organize emails and contacts).

The database for your email list can be part of a customer database you currently use, or it can be something entirely separate. That said, it's *critical* not to get confused about which customers (and prospective customers) have agreed to receive emails from you.

A contact form on your website is one of the most common ways to compile an email list. If you're having trouble getting visitors to fill out the form, some incentives can help: *Join our email list and receive 20 percent off your first purchase.*

Designing a great email

An effective email starts with the header. This includes the "From" line and address and the subject line.

The "From" line doesn't simply have to be your email address per se. You can set this up to read as your full name, or your company name, or both.

If another name (such as your website domain) might be more recognizable to people who have signed up for your emails, it's best to use this name. You don't want recipients to be confused about who's sending them emails.

The **subject line** is incredibly important, because this is the most information that will be provided before someone opens your email. It must compel the recipient to want to know more.

Subject line real estate is valuable, because most email providers only display the first 30 to 50 characters, and most mobile devices only show the first 20 to 30 characters. You need to get your point across concisely.

Normally this is where we'd suggest a strong sales pitch, but that could backfire in a more sensitive business such as deathcare services.

As with any professional communication, it's critical to spell words in your subject lines correctly and avoid spammy elements such as excessive punctuations (especially exclamation points), all-caps, capitalizing the first letter of every word, or using "Re:" (when it's not actually in response to anything).

Also, ambiguous or deceptive subject lines such as "Hi!" or "I've missed you" are always to be avoided (and would be inappropriate for cemetery marketing regardless).

Be sure to brand your emails with a consistent template or a consistent color scheme. Including your company's logo also is a must. It should look like what it is: a professional communication from a professional provider of deathcare services.

Visual elements: Marketing pros will tell you there are a lot of psychological elements you can use in your design to draw the eye where you want it to be. That's absolutely true, but it's beyond the scope of this book.

You should know the basics: Be sure the email is clear and easy to read. Be sure the most important aspects (particularly the call to action) are eye-catching and direct. Add visual anchors such as images (within reason) to break up the copy and make it appealing to read.

(Note on images: Without getting too technical, it's much better for your images to be referenced to a remote folder than embedded. Emails with embedded links are much more likely to be filtered as junk. A marketing expert can help you understand the difference.)

Content of your email

Be personable: As with your landing page copy, you don't want to sound too academic. Talk to your recipient the same way you'd talk to a visitor to your cemetery. Be professional, but you honestly don't have to be stuffy.

You want to contract with this person for a discussion about options you provide, and you're explaining why it will be beneficial to that person. Do so in a professional but friendly way.

Links: If you're not linking to your landing page or a page that's specific to your offer in your email, you're wasting a great opportunity. Even if your email is purely communicative, there's no reason not to provide a one-click opportunity to get more information on you and your business in the body of the email.

Use incentives: Every time you send an email, it should have a purpose. "Hey, I'm still here!" is not a purpose. Show your appreciation for people on your email list by offering them, for example, a limited-time discount. They're opening up their email boxes to you, so reward them for that.

An informational email works well, too: Maybe you're not looking to promote a particular service at this time. That's fine. Is there some information about the deathcare industry that would be (truly) interesting to your potential clientele? If so, that's enough reason for an email.

Don't waste people's time by sending these out constantly or for minor matters, but delivering useful information is a great way to stay in people's minds, along with a great excuse to include links to your website.

If you don't have the time or resources to create your own emails, there are lots of great copywriting services that can help you achieve your goals, and many are very reasonable.

Monitoring your email results

Again, I won't get into all the technical aspects here, but there are great services that will allow you to easily track your return on investment from business emails. They let you review lots of useful data, including:

- Which emails bounced
- Why they bounced
- Who opened the emails
- What links the recipient clicked
- Who unsubscribed
- Who forwarded your emails

This data can go a long way toward helping you refine your email marketing efforts and improving conversions.

There are more elements to successful email campaigns, but understanding these basics will help you determine the best way to use email to help your business succeed.

Email lists: Should you purchase them? (Spoiler alert: no.)

A precompiled email list sure sounds like a good deal when you're marketing your cemetery business. You have a list of emails for people who are prequalified to be interested in preplanning for burials or cremation. What could go wrong?

Um... just *everything*.

The first thing to remember is that even if you worked with an email list provider for a list that has been shaped to include only customers who meet certain demographic or psychographic (personality, interests, lifestyles, etc.) standards, *it's not really an opt-in list*.

No one opted in for communications regarding your services. The people on that email list simply opted in to an email communication from someone at some point in time (like the list provider).

When you're emailing people who haven't shown an interest in your business, that's something most people consider spamming — and you're not likely to see much return on those communications anyway.

Also, there's really no such thing as a good email list that's for sale. Typically, any addresses that once had value already have been spammed by a variety of other businesses.

Yes, there's that word again: **spam**. We're printing it in bold, even though we rarely do that (extra tip: use emphasis tools such as bold sparingly so they don't lose all meaning), because it's so important to understand that contacting people through a purchased email list almost always equates to spam.

If your business is defined as a spammer, your email deliverability and the reputation of your IP address almost certainly will be harmed. Organizations dedicated to combating email spam have a tool called a **honeypot**. It's a planted email address that, when emailed, identifies the sender as a spammer.

There are other spam traps that identify if an email address is old (or no longer valid) but still receives consistent traffic.

There are effective ways to build email lists through proper means. For the sake of your business and its reputation, don't go the purchased email route. The rewards are few and the risks are far too great.

Section 4: Monitoring and Measuring

CHAPTER 7
What Gets Measured Gets Done

Yes, "What gets measured gets done." It's a well-known saying, and properly so: it works. When you're constantly monitoring and measuring your results, you can determine what's working and what's not. You can find the places where you need to revise, tweak, or even go in an entirely new direction.

Here's the beautiful thing about today's digital world: Monitoring and measuring your marketing efforts is now incredibly fast, unbelievably precise, and unexpectedly easy.

Not only that, but you have far more flexibility now in what you do with the information you get from your analytics. You'll know what you need to do and be able to do exactly that on the fly.

You can make changes to your website that go live immediately. (Yes, it can take some time for spiders to crawl the site, but changes you make will be seen by human visitors right away.)

You can revise a PPC ad so that leads see the new information the very same day. When your analytics show that your customers are excited about a particular promotion, you can showcase it on social media.

Google Analytics

This is the best known and most popular of the user-friendly measuring tools, owing at least in part to the fact that so many businesses use Google advertising and other services.

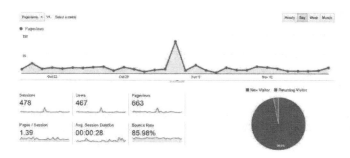

In essence, Google Analytics generates detailed statistics about a website's traffic and traffic sources, along with measuring conversions and sales. This makes it an incredibly useful tool for marketers and business owners. The basic service is free, but there's a premium option available for a fee.

The service can track visitors from a broad variety of sources, including search engines, social networks, direct visits, and referring sites. It also displays advertising, pay-per-click networks, email marketing, and digital collateral such as links within PDF documents.

Google Analytics is completely integrated with Google Ads, making it easy to review online campaigns by tracking landing page quality and conversions.

Target goals can include sales, lead generation, viewing a specific page, or downloading a particular file, among other options.

Some of the many things you can analyze

Whether you use Google Analytics or another site-monitoring tool — the former is practically a requirement, and other tools are best used in combination with Google Analytics — here are some of the many things you can monitor:

- **Number of visits**

- **Number of people who actually visited your site:** A person may visit your site more than once, and each time, that's a separate visit.

- **Number of pages per visit:** Each time a person visits your site, the visitor might view a single page or go on to view dozens of them. (If you've populated your site with great content, hopefully the visitor is reviewing it in detail.) The greater the number of pages viewed per visit, the more people are actually exploring the information it contains.

- **List of most visited pages:** This indicates the number of visits received by each individual page. You can then use this list to analyze which themes, products, and information grab your customers' attention the most. It also includes your campaign landing pages, providing you with final statistics for each of your marketing initiatives.

- **Length of stay:** This indicates how long on average your visitors stayed on your site, thus indicating how well they relate to your content. The longer your visitors stay, the greater their interest. This gets to the issue of **bounce rate**, which I'll touch on in a moment.

- **Origin of visitors:** This identifies what site someone was viewing on the internet immediately before visiting your site. Think of it like a flight: One city's airport is the place of departure; the other is the place of arrival. It's beneficial to know where your visitor arrived from — that makes it much easier to know what prompted them to check out your business.

- These origin statistics can show **direct visits**, in which customers enter your URL directly into the browser; **site referrals**, in which a visitor comes to your site after clicking on a link at another website, a **blog** or **social media network**; and **search engines results pages**.

Tracking phone calls

Businesses that mostly do e-commerce and sell products and services online aren't so concerned with phone calls. They do the vast majority of their business digitally.

In fact, many products are sold online without any direct involvement by the person selling them. An automated purchasing system is set up, the customer purchases the item, and it's automatically delivered digitally (if not a physical item) or goes into a queue to be delivered from a drop-shipper or wholesaler.

For a business such as yours, of course, it's an entirely different story. While you might (and should) get inquiries by email or through a form on your website, many inquiries for prearrangements will be coming in over the phone.

Sure, some hair salons have online registration systems, just like restaurants have online reservations (either on their own site or through an app such as Open Table) and many other service providers.

And there's no question that in 2021, millennials are *far more comfortable* handling their business digitally as they are over the phone. Some are more comfortable doing it that way.

But when looking at all demographics, even today most people making an appointment with a local business do so over the phone.

That's particularly true in an industry such as deathcare, where such obviously are of a more personal nature. Making arrangements for a recently passed family member is the sort of thing one does in person or over the phone. (Of course, there's also Skype, videoconferencing and other types of real-time chat, but I'll stick with the basics here.) This is why understanding how to track phone calls that originate from your website is so important.

Many people now make phone calls simply by clicking on a link. When they do it on a desktop computer, typically they have it set up to call through Skype or some other VoIP (**voice over Internet Protocol**) service.

These days, however, many more people will be visiting your website — or your Google My Business page, or your Yelp listing, your Facebook Business page, a PPC ad, etc. — on a digital device that's *also* a phone.

Because your phone number is also a link that allows people to call you with a click, they can contact you *immediately* directly from your listing. The easier you make it for the lead to contact you, the better.

That's why having a *clickable* phone number (just like a clickable email address) everywhere you have a Web presence is so important.

When your phone number is clickable, an experienced internet marketing pro can easily track phone calls made from your site and listings. You can see how many leads are coming directly from your site in the form of phone calls (emails also are easily tracked, as you might assume).

You can see what times of the day the site is most effective in getting phone leads, how long people visited the site before calling, what page they were viewing before they called, and so on. This lets you optimize your site to convert the most traffic into leads.

Bounce rate and site engagement

As I indicated earlier, in 2021, your website can't merely exist because "everybody has one." It's not just there to display some elegant pictures of your cemetery, along with some basic contact information.

Your website needs to be *actively engaging* its visitors. It must be designed to communicate trustworthiness, engage the visitor, sell the visitor that you're the best solution to a particular problem, and convert the visitor into a customer.

You can implement all the best practices toward creating an engaging, high-converting site, but only through analytics will you know how well it's working — and which aspects of the site are delivering the conversions (and which are not).

The first thing most experts focus on when assessing site engagement is the **bounce rate**. Though the definition for this can vary a bit, I'll stick with the Google Analytics definition: It's the percentage of visits in which the visitor only views *one page* before leaving the site.

For certain businesses, having a high bounce rate isn't a terrible thing; they might be trying to communicate something very simple with a very basic single landing page. They might not even have more than one page on the site. That's probably true of many of your local competitors' sites, and it might be true of yours.

Bounce rate can be broken down in many ways, including factoring which visitor origins have the highest bounce rate and which have the lowest.

The other concern regarding bounce rates relates to SEO: Google and other search engines take your bounce rate into account when ranking you. It's another key reason to design your site in a way that invites the visitor to stick around and check out additional content.

Reducing bounce rate

If you've set up your site in a legitimate manner with white-hat SEO, and at least spread some solid content across several pages, you don't have to worry about the worst bounce rate percentages.

Those terrible numbers typically are reserved for sites that attract visitors through misleading (black-hat) means.

They persuade people to click through to the site by implying there is a diamond in the stocking when they click through, but what the visitor finds is a lump of coal. The visitor immediately clicks out of the site, which is why bounce rate is such a major factor in search engine rankings.

Still, the better the bounce rate, the better for your business. Ways to improve your bounce rate include:

Browser/mobile compatibility: If your site isn't optimized for mobile devices, you'll get *a lot* of bounces from visitors trying to access it on phones. Also, be sure your site displays properly on all the major browsers — especially Google Chrome, the industry leader.

Pay off your ads on your site: When someone reads an ad that promises one thing, but clicks through to discover another, that's a quick bounce. Be sure your site is set up logically and intuitively, and be sure your site delivers exactly what your ads promise.

Don't annoy the visitor: If you hit the visitor with pop-up ads, chat windows, a blatant call to action, and more right on the landing page, kiss that visitor goodbye. It's quite obvious that a cemetery site with a tacky interface is going to put off potential clientele in no time flat.

Keep your landing page attractive and welcoming. Let the visitor feel "at home" and interested in exploring before placing demands. It never hurts to think of a virtual visitor as a guest in your home.

Check your page load times: If your site uses extremely complicated design or lots of graphics, some pages could take a while to load — this is a known factor in high bounce rates.

You can test page load times through analytics. If your pages are taking substantially longer than average, it's time to do some redesign.

There are ways to streamline the mobile version of your site so that large files, for example, do not automatically display.

The visitor can be provided an option to display these files if desired, which might be the case, for example, if the visitor is viewing the site on a tablet or large-display smartphone over Wi-Fi.

Improve your content: This is a general tip, but it's one of the most important. Small things such as spelling and grammatical errors can cause a visitor to lose faith in your business and bounce out. So can something that could be considered polarizing, such as political statement. High-quality content returns low bounce rates. Low-quality content returns high bounce rates.

The five basic traffic metrics

When analyzing your site's traffic, there are five basic metrics to understand:

Sessions: A session is another word for a single visit. It's one person visiting your site any one time. If someone visits your site 15 times, those visits count as 15 sessions, whether she stayed on the site for 5 minutes or 50.

Unique visitors: A unique visitor is one person visiting your site any number of times during a defined period. If someone visits your site eight times in a week, that person still counts as one unique visitor.

Page views: A single page view is any one visitor viewing one page of your site, one time. The page must have a unique address (URL). If someone visits your landing page and then clicks a link to your About Us page, those are two page views.

Time on site: This is the total amount of time one visitor spends on your site in the course of a single session. Average time on site is a critical measure of visit quality and visitor interest.

Referrers: If someone clicks a search result link to reach your site, the point of origin — the departure airport I talked about earlier — is known as the referrer.

There are many ways in which a marketing professional can use these metrics to help improve your site's traffic and conversions, but the details go somewhat beyond the scope of this book.

What's critical to understand regarding monitoring and measuring is the digital age lets you precisely understand every aspect of your site's effectiveness and your marketing campaign — and it lets you make virtually instantaneous changes to optimize your efforts.

Knowing which referrers tend to send the most traffic your way can help you decide where to focus your marketing and promotional efforts.

Of course, it's just as important to know how well visitors are converting who arrive from particular referrers — another statistic that can be easily mined from the data.

Analytics essentially provide you honest feedback on all your efforts. People might tell you they like one thing or another, but the proof is in how long they spend on a page, what they choose to click on, whether they decide to move forward and convert to a customer. The digital age lets you see all that information in a way that can power your success.

Section 5:
Working with a
Marketing Professional

CHAPTER 8
Finding a Qualified, Principled (Internet) Marketing Professional

You know why I put internet in parentheses: Because as I've noted several times before, internet marketing is virtually synonymous with marketing in 2021 and going forward.

However, many marketers remain behind the 8-ball when it comes to understanding how to promote their companies online.

You'll want to find a company that specializes in online marketing, but it's just as important to be sure the company uses appropriate methods that will keep you on the good side of Google, other search engines, and laws regarding spam and legitimate marketing methods.

But this consideration is most important of all: You want to work with **full-stack marketing agency**.

What does that mean?

I'm glad you asked.

The short version is that you want a marketing agency that can do it all, that has a wide spectrum of "weapons" in its arsenal and can employ them as needed.

One approach most definitely does not fit all when marketing cemeteries. Different firms have different needs, different budgets, different goals.

They have different levels of competition in their particular areas. Speaking of areas, the geography of a particular cemetery plays a big role in which marketing methods will work best.

Some agencies don't do PPC advertising at all. Some don't do remarketing. Or hyper-geotargeting. Or review and reputation optimization. Or website conversions optimization.

A (frankly shocking) number of agencies are happy to take your money and add your cemetery to their "one-size-fits-all solution." And honestly, it doesn't work.

It's also true that you don't want to waste money on marketing services you don't need — or don't fit your particular goals at the time.

A reputable full-stack agency has all the options available, but it *also* won't try to pad its wallet by requiring you to accept a "full suite of services" if some make zero sense for your particular situation.

Instead, a legitimate agency will take the time to understand your exact situation and work *with* you to create a campaign that includes the services with the best ROI and most effectiveness for you.

When scrutinizing a marketing agency, first make sure it effectively employs all the tools listed in this book. Then make sure the agency will *specifically customize a plan* that works best for *you*, employing all the tools *you* need — but none that you don't.

That's how reputable agencies work.

Using an internet marketing pro vs. doing it yourself

In many ways, we now live in a DIY society, and that's a good thing. With the expansion of 24/7 internet access into people's homes, we now have a wealth of information at our fingertips any time of day.

It's like having access to hundreds of thousands of libraries at all times, right there in your office, or living room, or porch, or wherever.

You can take your smartphone to the beach and access 100,000 times more information than a person could at the largest big-city library 25 years ago.

All of that information makes it much easier for people to solve their own problems. Need tips for changing the pedals on your bicycle? There are not only step-by-step guides on the internet, but YouTube videos as well — and they're all completely free.

Some businesses take this approach for their internet marketing efforts. While a few are successful at this, that's generally because the business is related to internet marketing, or something closely affiliated with it, in the first place.

For most business owners, the best use of your time is doing what you do well. You handle deathcare services, which is a very specific focus. You know how to work with individuals and families regarding delicate subjects.

That's a lot on your plate. You should be focused on your clients and your services, not trying to determine which keyword phrase gets you the best PPC results.

You should be ensuring that a complicated burial service went exactly as planned, not figuring out how to edit image tags in your website code to improve your search engine rankings.

The DIY route might make sense if employing the right internet marketing firm were extremely expensive, but it's not. Some great firms are very affordable, and the increase in business will pay for the initiative many times over.

When it comes to justifying the cost, also consider this: Truly great marketing will help you become more selective.

The more potential clients or customers you have, the choosier you can be. If you only have 10 clients (but can handle 25), you might have to undersell your services, because you can't risk losing the 10 clients you have. However, if you have 50 people who want to use your services, you can set your prices at a much more appropriate rate.

You're well aware of how direct cremation providers have driven down the expected costs of services among consumers. You don't want to have to wrangle with price shoppers all the time.

It's good to be selective. At Ring Ring Marketing, quite frankly, *I'm* selective. Virtually every week, I turn down the opportunity to work a potential client or two.

If the numbers won't work for my business, it doesn't make sense to take on the campaign. (Remember, we have a 100 percent money-back guarantee, so we're taking on all the risk.)

I also turn down a potential client if that cemetery's particular situation means it's unlikely to see a great benefit from our campaigns. I'm not in the business of taking people's money. I'm in the business of helping cemeteries grow and succeed. Nothing less is considered a successful partnership to me.

Red flags to watch out for when choosing an internet marketing firm

Now that you know the benefits of hiring a professional to handle your internet marketing, you need to know how to select one. The skills, experience, resources, and customer support abilities of various firms can vary widely from one to another.

Here I'll touch on additional "red flags" that are indicative of the way certain internet marketing consultants, particularly those with large firms, do business. I'll follow each one with a short explanation of how a legitimate business would handle the situation.

RED FLAG #1:
Conflicts of Interest

The problem with many large internet marketing firms is that while they are managing your campaign, they are also managing your direct competitors' campaigns.

You and your competitors all are competing for presence on the first page of search engine results. The space is limited. Whose interest does the firm have in mind?

In addition, at a big firm, your account representative is hired to sell — not to manage your campaign. How can he manage your campaign if he's pressured by his managers to hit sales goals every week? The rep's incentive is to sell, not to generate more sales for you.

If he triples your sales, he doesn't benefit it any way. If fact, if he ignores your account, he actually makes *more* money, because he's using the time he *should* be helping you to "close" more clients. Your account gets neglected and performance suffers.

At a legit marketing firm, your dedicated account manager is a dedicated marketing professional (at RRM, we call them *coaches*, because that's a big part of their role), not a salesperson. The managers are under no pressure to go out and find accounts. Their sole purpose is the continual optimization of your campaign, to bring in customers and make your phone ring.

They have top-level technical expertise in internet marketing and have helped numerous businesses — including cemeteries — transform leads from online to your phone line.

RED FLAG #2
Lack of transparency

Most companies doing great work want to illustrate what they can achieve. That means sharing all the numbers with their customers. However, many large internet marketing firms do not provide you with all the data associated with your campaigns.

For example, they do not show you what exact keywords they bid on, which match type they use, what the bounce rate is, or the quality score associated with each keyword.

Those terms might be unfamiliar, but they're easily explained by a quality consultant. You don't need to know what all these words mean, but you do need to know that these are the words that measure whether a campaign is actually working.

A good internet marketer will not shy away from providing you a result with all this information. When you do good work for a customer, you want to show it off. You want your customers to know exactly what you're achieving for them. When that information is hidden, you have no way to know.

It's equivalent to FedEx sharing its percentage rates for on-time arrivals. These are the key numbers that measure whether your marketing is succeeding or failing.

At a legit marketing firm, all the data is shared with you. The company should share with you exactly what it has done with your campaign every week. If a company does good work, why would it do anything else?

RED FLAG #3
Retention through contracts, not by results

A number of large internet marketing firms require contracts with minimum term commitments. Why is that a concern? It relates to how internet marketing works.

Business owners generally will know within 2–3 months whether their marketing provider is achieving the results they'd been promised. Unfortunately, if they want to terminate their campaign when they have a minimum term commitment, they're out of luck. Whether the campaign is soaring or nosediving, the business owner is on the hook.

If you're providing real, quantifiable results every month, why require a minimum term?

At a legit marketing firm, programs run month to month. Most partners see results in 30 days, but sometimes it takes 2–3 months, depending on the particular market.

After that time frame, you can terminate the service if you like. However, after 90 days, customers typically are so thrilled with the results that they don't want to leave. They've achieved tremendous growth in their revenue and want to keep that going.

RED FLAG #4
Lack of technical knowledge

A lot of large internet marketing firms do not actually employ internet marketing experts.

They employ — as you'll remember from a few pages back — salespeople.

When you sign on with these firms, the person managing your pay-per-click campaign is not a marketing pro. It's your account representative.

Here's the problem: She's a salesperson, not a marketing technical engineer.

These account reps undergo a few weeks of crash training and are expected to manage your campaign. In fact, they are not certified.

Internet marketing is a very complicated process, and most salespeople are not very good at it. They earn their pay by being good at sales, not internet marketing.

At a legit marketing firm, your dedicated account manager is a dedicated marketing engineer. The managers' sole purpose is to *optimize* your campaign and help you generate more sales and higher revenue.

Unlike larger companies that check in on your account once a week, a legit company will actively manage your account on a daily basis. It will monitor and adjust your campaign every day to achieve the outcome you and the expert decided upon together.

Once the firm has a great pay-per-click campaign set up for you, it can make sure it's always achieving results by working continuously to improve it.

Your target market's keywords might change every month. Your competition might suddenly be paying more for same keywords, lowering your ad position. Perhaps your competition comes up with an ad that has a better offer — your ads still show, but fewer people click on them.

Continuous management is essential to keeping your online advertising costs down. That's what a good firm does.

RED FLAG #5
Focusing on the number of ad clicks, rather than on your business

With many large internet marketing firms, it's in their best interest to drive more clicks and spend all your budget each month, then come back to ask you to spend even more. The company makes its money based on the percentage of your spending.

If that sounds ridiculous to you, well, it does to me too. You're paying good money to drive customers to your website. It is critical that these visitors *go on to call your business*.

These companies do not do any website conversion optimization to ensure that traffic turns into customers. They only care about delivering traffic to your website, not to your phone line.

Here's the problem with that: If your website isn't optimized in the first place — if it has a hard-to-find phone number, no offer, etc. — no amount of traffic will save you.

The primary purpose of the website is to create contact by phone or email. Optimizing your website for this purpose is a vital part of this process.

At a legit marketing firm, it all comes down to the bottom line: delivering a high return on investment. That means turning website visitors into sales.

Conversion rate optimization is an ongoing process of testing and tuning your website to make your phone ring. A good firm teaches you how to fine-tune your site to convert more online visitors into sales.

Conclusions

Staying ahead in a digital world

I've covered a lot of information in this book, and I realize it's a lot to take in.

Even without digging into all the minutiae of various marketing efforts in a digital world, as you can see, it's a very different battlefield than companies dealt with five years ago, or even two years ago.

I could tell you that everything will reach a nice, level plateau for a while, that once you understand how successful business marketing works in a digital world, that you'll be up on the status quo for the next several years.

But that isn't true.

The one constant of successful business marketing today is that nothing is constant. Social media networks that were incredibly influential at the start of this decade (I'm looking at you, MySpace — and you, Friendster) are virtually extinct today.

Mobile phones that were cutting-edge a few years ago can't handle the vast majority of applications that are most used today.

Websites that attracted tons of traffic and converted visitors almost automatically are useless today (if they haven't been updated since then).

It all sounds scary, but in truth, the ever-changing influence of technology on local businesses in this digital age is a very *good* thing — for those willing to adapt and use it to their benefit.

These circumstances provide business owners who can adjust on the fly in 2021 an enormous advantage over local competitors who are still doing business the 2015 way, much less the 2010 way.

I feel fortunate to have worked with lots of great deathcare professionals like you. I've seen firsthand how much more revenue they can generate by employing the very same tools I cover in this book.

These tools allow small business owners to separate themselves completely from the pack. They can attract and target prospective customers long before their competitors are even aware of them. They can evaluate and measure their marketing approaches on the fly and improve them with virtually no delay.

Yes, things move fast these days. No, it will never be as simple as it was to simply run a local business. But that's simply the reality.

Times change, and people who accept that change and adapt to it will thrive. Those who do not, no matter how good they are at what they do, will stagnate and die off.

Perhaps that doesn't seem fair, and that's understandable. If you're the best in your location at providing cemetery services, shouldn't that be all that matters? You do a great job at a fair price. All business should naturally flow to you.

In truth, that's never been the case. Simply being good at your chosen vocation might be enough if you're an employee, but you're not an employee.

You're a business owner. You took the plunge to be enterprising and run your own business, and that's wonderful. And as the owner, you know that whatever you do that running the business side is its own discipline, one that's very different than simply product sales and installation.

That discipline *did* change long before now.

It changed with the advent of websites and email. It changed when payroll went from being calculated with pencils and erasers to Excel spreadsheets. It changed when you went from contacting employees on pagers and walkie-talkies to mobile phones.

Things are just changing faster now. Much, much faster. And it's not just the speed of things — it's also how far their influence has spread demographically. Incredibly powerful technology is in the palm of people's hands, and they're using it. Every age, every race, everywhere.

It doesn't matter if you're in the heart of a big city or working in a small town. Your potential customers are employing this technology in their day-to-day lives, and it's only going to become more pervasive.

This doesn't mean you need to become a master of the digital world. You can run your cemetery and focus on what you do best. I've worked with lots of small business owners who just wanted the phone to ring.

And that's what I do. I employ the techniques in this book, in addition to other methods, as necessary, to attract visitors, to convert those visitors into customers, to make a business's phone ring off the hook.

The business owner can be as involved or removed as he or she likes. Some proprietors want to know and help control every aspect of the process. We can do that. Some want to be almost entirely hands-off. We can do that too. And anything in between? Never a problem.

That's because you know best how to run your cemetery. You know your strengths and weaknesses. You know what requires your direct supervision and what you can delegate. The same thing works with marketing in the digital world.

You can figure out what works best for you. A qualified marketing expert will adjust to your needs and expectations. The only important thing is making your phone ring.

Having read this book, you might think you need to employ all these marketing aspects immediately. On the other hand, it might sound so overwhelming, you might think it's best to ignore them altogether.

It should be obvious that the second option isn't an option at all. Other small businesses are employing these initiatives. They are getting more bang for their buck, expanding their customer bases, and identifying the best and most profitable customers, using these methods.

With that said, your cemetery doesn't necessarily need to do everything that's listed here. It depends on what you do. It depends on your budget. It depends on what resources are best directed to provide you the very best return on your investment.

Various marketing companies do things different ways. My company offers a 100 percent money-back guarantee, because we know what we do works. We know how to attract people who are looking for exactly what you provide.

Really, we're just like you: We're good at what we do, and we want to share our expertise with local businesses and help them grow.

Things move fast in the business marketing world, and I don't expect the proprietors I partner with to stay up on these things. That's what *I* handle.

I stay apprised of every twist and turn and use that knowledge to benefit my partners. That's what a good marketing expert should do. It ensures that my clients stay ahead of the game, and it's a game that changes month to month, sometimes week to week.

Now that you've learned the basics of marketing in today's digital world, take some time to assess your marketing efforts and how they've been working for you.

Do you know how effective your advertising is?

Do you know what customers are saying about your cemetery online, in user reviews, in ratings, and on social media?

Do you know whether people can easily access your website on smartphones?

Do you know whether your cemetery even shows up on Google Maps or Apple Maps?

If you don't know the answer to these questions off the top of your head, it's probably time to take a long look at how you're marketing your business in a digital age.

Business owners who know the answers to these questions are highly visible to potential customers. Those who don't are typically flying way under the radar. You can't afford to be off that radar.

I want to thank you for taking the time to read this book and consider the points I've discussed here. If you're looking for more information on marketing your business in the digital age, I'll be more than happy to speak with you. Here are a few ways to get in touch:

Contact me anytime through email at:
welton@ringringmarketing.com

Visit our website for cemetery owners:
www.RingRingMarketing.com

Call us toll-free:
(888) 383-2848

Thanks again, and let me wish you and your business great success now and for many years to come.

Welton Hong

Ring Ring Marketing Information

Ring Ring Marketing only makes money when our clients make money. Our work produces amazing results, so we stand behind it with a <u>60-day no-questions-asked money-back guarantee</u>.

We have a simple evaluation process for businesses interested in partnering with us. We'll discuss your particular company and how we can employ an online marketing campaign structured specifically for you.

Because we specialize in the cemetery industry, we know exactly how to design a campaign we know will be successful for you.

If the numbers don't work out and we're unable to help you, it won't cost you a penny. That's why there's <u>zero risk</u> in contacting us for an evaluation. We want to make it easy for you.

Now is the time to act. You simply can't afford to get left behind. Learn how a professionally executed internet marketing campaign can make this your most successful year ever.

Visit our website for cemetery owners:
www.RingRingMarketing.com

Call us toll-free: **(888) 383-2848**

Made in the USA
Columbia, SC
03 April 2022